<re>Relate

Nidal Humoee

RIVER BIRCH PRESS

Mesa, Arizona

ISBN 978-1-956365-67-2 (print)
ISBN 978-1-956365-68-9 (e-book)

For Worldwide Distribution
Printed in the U.S.A.

River Birch Press
P.O. Box 7341, Mesa, AZ 85216

CONTENTS

ACKNOWLEDGMENTS

Writing a book is a significant time investment. It is a risky yet rewarding endeavor. Being a physician means I have little free time available, if ever. I needed plenty of discipline. Halfway into the work, a software glitch caused the loss of months worth of writing. This time, I needed an outpouring of grace to restart from scratch. Clawing my way back, I eventually finished the book draft.

I am indebted to many for their support, but mainly to two individuals whose inspiration was foundational: My friend Philip Stephano, and my own brother, Haytham Hamwi. Both affirmed, at different times, their belief in my ability to handle this delicate assignment.

To my delight, my kids, John and Jack, never shied off reading and giving great feedback while my gifted daughter, Jianna, helped design the diagrams of the four lenses. I would like to thank my longtime friend Kelly for her kind listening and calm demeanor during moments of frustration.

The book draft would not have seen the light or taken the shape of relatable content without author and literary agent Keith Carroll. His keen insight and thoughtfulness were instrumental. I would also like to thank Brian and Kathy at the River Birch Press for their talent and dedication.

Many thanks to all of my amazing friends who carved time out of their busy lives to read and provide truthful endorsements.

My final words of gratitude go to Dr. Henry Cloud, Dr. John Townsend, Dr. David Augsburger, Joyce Meyer, and other writers. Their books undoubtedly fueled growth within me and many others.

FOREWORD

In this concise, deeply personal, and profoundly insightful book, Dr. Humoee focuses his talents for healing on a matter of singular importance to our times: the restoration of healthy personal attitudes. The downstream effects of corrupt attitudes can be seen in epidemics of depression, identity crisis, addiction, conflict, and increasing cynicism in our society.

Following the pattern of Christ and in the spirit of Luke the physician and disciple, Dr. Humoee provides a practical and accessible approach to restoring personhood, healing dysfunctional relationships, and living life abundantly.

If the reader finds, as I did, that this is more than just another self improvement book, it is because the heart of Christ is at the center of Dr. Humoee's purpose. We are fortunate to have this book for such a time as this.

Philip Stephano
Pipersville, PA

PREFACE

Have you gushed over someone but weren't sure how to demonstrate that? When Jesus reclined in Simon's home, Mary lavished on him an extravagant scent. She could have elegantly wrapped the gift and presented it. But Mary demonstrated her love in an unrestrained, communicative way. She anointed Jesus' feet with the perfume using nothing but her hair! Her attitude was refreshing to Jesus, who praised it and said it would be talked about by everyone everywhere.

When you have an honorable attitude, you do not need fancy gifts. You become a gift to others. Imagine the excitement!

Jesus declared us to be the salt of the earth. We often use salt shakers to sprinkle salt deliberately. Your attitude resembles the salt shaker. It allows you to conduct yourself in a way that values others, invites responsibility, and accepts their differences. When treated this way, others will feel more heard, known, and loved.

In applying sound attitudes or lenses, you will be better able to distinguish the trustworthiness of others with whom you can enjoy intimacy, acceptance, and fulfillment. The lenses magnify responsibility lines, making it straightforward to delegate responsibility and avoid frustration and micromanagement!

The sound lenses enable us to honor others and confront them simultaneously. We resolve conflicts more often and feel more equal and reconciled in family, church, and community.

Distorted attitudes derail relationships, igniting offense and strife, culminating in a tidal emotional wave of sadness, fear, and anger. It eventually corrals us into a corner of despair and loneliness.

The importance of the attitude is far-reaching; it influences how we relate to God, education, and business partners.

Re-relate invites responsibility for attitudes and realigning them with principles of love, freedom, and equality. Abundant emotional life is not a dream but attainable to those who seek it.

INTRODUCTION

Stuck in traffic, I read a bumper sticker that said, "Just be nice." I muttered, "I wish it were that simple!" My attitude has always been nice enough, in my view anyway.

Let's consider our daily routines. We meet family and friends, go to our job, and afterwards head to a fitness class or a grocery store. In these activities, we conduct ourselves and perceive others' conduct through our attitude.

In his letter to the Corinthians, the Apostle Paul praises faith, hope, and love. When we think about them, we can see that they are relational experiences between us, God, and others.

What if something happens that causes us to realize that we may need to learn a different way of going about relationships—in other words, begin to relate to others in a different way? It happened to me in the aftermath of a failed relationship when I petitioned God to help me pick up the pieces and begin to relate differently with others—what I call Re-Relate.

As a result, I have poured the new insights I received into this book. *Re-Relate* focuses on attitudes we use to interpret our interactions with others and refers to these attitudes as relational lenses. It chronicles the formation of these lenses of bonding, distinctness, integration, and levelness, which we will explain further in the book. But when our relational lenses are distorted, they lead us to relate to others in offensive ways.

Re-Relate applies these relational lenses to shed light on the dynamic processes of trust, dialogue, and conflict in the midst of our forgiving and reconciling with others.

In Matthew 6:22, Jesus describes the eye as the lamp of the body. Soiled lenses block the light that helps us see clearly, inevitably causing us to stumble. On the other hand, clear relational lenses let the light in, enabling us to walk in love and perceive others as worthy—a noble life indeed.

Being God's offspring, we perceive Him through sound relational lenses as forgiving, gracious, and truthful, and therefore we should reflect his true image to others. In contrast, when we use distorted lenses, we perceive a God who abandons, degrades, and condemns us. We also reflect this false image to others even as we tell them about his goodness and mercy!

Re-Relate will broaden your insight to love deeper, abide in God more, and hope better. You don't have to settle for anything less than the abundant life God desires for you.

1

Taking Boundaries Personally

Becoming Conscious of Self

Sitting in my aging leather recliner, I sighed as my kittens watched me intently. Thoughts of my recent broken relationship kept invading my mind, and of how my ex's stepfather had mistreated her when she was growing up. Since he was therefore out of the picture to help her through the trauma of our breakup, was there anyone else available? How was she managing it all? A heavy feeling of dread engulfed me even though I no longer had any responsibility for her or commitment to her.

My therapist has been keen on telling me I need to take care of myself, but I have had trouble doing so. I know it is good to be concerned about others, but now I was also getting the message that I needed to first concentrate on getting myself to a good place before I could begin to help others.

I picked up my phone and opened the Bible app. Clicking the play button, I heard the words from the psalmist playing gently in my ears: "You desire the truth in my innermost being" (Psalm 51:6).

Suddenly, it hit me. The truth is that my ex-girlfriend is not my most inner thing—she is *not* me. We are distinct. Her thoughts don't belong to me. Her family's hurts are not mine. So why did I rehearse them over and over in the last few days and react to them as if they were mine? Was I attempting to take care of her troubles so that she would love me? I grabbed my journal to write. I couldn't wait until I met my therapist to share these new thoughts.

My therapist told me that I was a loving person, but that I have injured boundaries and let others overwhelm me. I didn't recognize what was in me. I was not conscious of self, and as such, I didn't take care of myself properly.

That afternoon I determined to begin to focus my thinking on myself to see where I was in life. I thought of it as taking my first personal inventory. But I have to be honest—it was terrible! My thoughts were scattered, twisted, and contradictory. The chaos in my head resembled taking inventory after a tornado—destruction was everywhere.

I began to journal about my feelings daily so I could handle them properly. I needed to decide which were legitimate and which I had no reason holding onto if I were in the business of personal growth. This was my first step towards erecting boundaries in my thought life. I continued for weeks and started feeling lighter.

I prayed earnestly for God to help me learn to care for myself. Not soon after this prayer, my tax accountant invited me to her Bible study where I learned much that helped me understand my true value. I took a course on learning to swim, ticking off one of those boxes I always had on hold. One day I noticed that my backyard was messy and riddled with weeds and crabgrass, so I hired someone that week to remove them and plant fresh herbs. My garden began blossoming, both literally and figuratively.

What Lies Inside

Our boundaries paint the outline of our intellectual and emotional portrait. With their help, we define the edges of our soul. Our soul exists inside the body and relies on it to receive and give information about situations and people around us. Nonetheless, we are spiritual creatures, and our soul is also linked with our spirit.

The soul contains the mind, emotions, and will. Those contents should occupy proportional space with one another. When they don't, for example, and our feelings flood past their designated area, they can overwhelm our will and cause us to act impulsively.

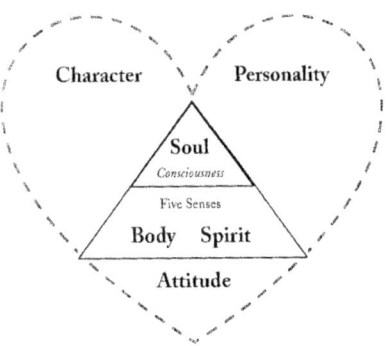

From Keith Carrol's book, Created to Relate, *with permission*

1. Mind

The mind contains thoughts that can be facts or perceptions. A fact is a physical event witnessed or heard while a perception is an inference we develop when interacting with another person. We use our perceptions to decipher relational situations.

Both facts and perceptions produce emotions. We feel fear in response to a physical threat or a relational interaction we view as threatening. We form our perceptions through early life experiences with our parents and others. Those perceptions eventually shape the attitudes we use to connect with others. In the same way that we put on glasses to read the news or social media, so too we put on our relational lenses to examine our relational interactions. Through those lenses, we connect with and feel about God and others.

Through receiving ample love deposits from God and our parents, we form *four sound relational lenses:* bonding, distinctness, integration, and levelness. In contrast, in the absence of love deposits, we perceive ourselves to be unworthy. As a result, we see others through *four deformed lenses:* abandonment, devaluation, splitting, and disparity lenses. We will go through each of these in detail in the chapters to come.

Whether sound or deformed, we are constantly using our relational lenses to interact with others and God. They are also how we perceive ourselves.

Our defective perceptions can be unnoticeable to us. God and our loved ones many times come to the rescue by speaking their truthful feedback about us being worthy and equal. We need patience and forbearance to receive the truth they share with us so that we can displace our distorted perceptions. This is how we kick-start our journey of emotional healing.

God is not a magician. He is a Spirit, and we need his Holy Spirit to discern his thoughts.

The person without the Spirit does not accept the things that come from the Spirit of God but considers them foolishness, and cannot understand them because they are discerned only through the Spirit (1 Corinthians 2:14).

He imparts His perceptions to our minds, leaving us to decide whether to receive them or not. God's first declaration to us when we approach Him is how much He loves us. God loved us first so that we could love (1 John 4:19). As we respond to God's love, our relational lenses begin to be transformed.

2. Emotions

We produce emotions in response to thoughts. The thought can be a perception, event, or memory. Emotions are energies, and once generated, they do not vanish easily. To deal with them, we should verbalize what we feel to both our trusted friends and God in order to receive understanding and empathy and not to condemn others. Non-verbalized emotions can influence our countenance by spilling out through our vocal inflection, facial expression, and body posture. Listeners feel us before decoding our words.

In the normal emotional response, we feel the emotion and confess its presence and intensity. We review the triggering thoughts and relate them together. In the midst of this, we may experience changes in our bodily functions such as faster heartbeats and breathing. Finally, we verbalize the emotion when it is feasible.

Emotions don't ethically contaminate our character because, contrary to motives, they are morally neutral. They are not wicked nor righteous. They, more importantly, inform us about the true nature of our perceptions. Embracing our feelings helps us interpret our perceived threats, demands, and achievements.

Here is a quick example. I feel angry when a colleague interrupts me at a committee meeting. I recognize anger as a demand to be heard. I calmly tell my colleague that I want to be heard.

Embracing emotions is not an invitation to act impulsively on them. We learn self-control by containing our emotions until we can divulge them to trustworthy listeners or write them in a journal. Proverbs 16:32 praises such a person: "Better a patient person than a warrior, one with self-control than one who takes a city."

It is wise to employ logic and emotions when making decisions. If our decisions happen to be incorrect, we can at least congratulate ourselves on making decisions with a complete set of tools at our disposal.

3. Will

We use our will to choose and to execute. Apart from emotional impulsivity, the use of our will is guided by motives, faith, and prior life experiences.

God's character is *loving* (1 John 4.8), *just* (2 Thessalonians 1:6), *holy* (1 Peter 1:16), and *righteous* (Psalm 7:11). Once we are born of Him, His Spirit imparts His perceptions on our minds. If we agree with, rehearse, and act on them, they become our moral motives.

Motives are translated through the relational lenses into social behavior toward others. For example, when we obey the love motive, we translate it through the levelness lens into acts of cherishing others as worthy and equal. Verbalizing our intentions to clarify misunderstandings is helpful, like Paul addressed believers in 1 Thessalonians 2:3: "The appeal we make does not spring from error or impure motives, nor we are trying to trick you." We should never assume we absolutely know others' motives. Instead, it is better to invite them to state their intentions.

Let's look at Kevin's relationship with Angelina, another example that is riddled with ineffective communication. One recent night, Kevin made coarse remarks about Angelina's dress. Angelina waged an utter war of silence for days. Eventually, she broke her silence and told Kevin via an email that he was no longer allowed in her house.

Remembering how she had always said she would never leave him, Kevin made the decision to dismiss what she had communicated in her email. He went out and purchased some flowers and headed to her residence. He felt unsure yet hopeful. To his dismay, Angelina called the police to escort him away.

Kevin felt confused and embarrassed. He decided to attend counseling to better understand where he went wrong. Slowly, he comprehended the risk of assuming he knew Angelina's intentions.

We should give great attention to the process of making choices because we spend long seasons experiencing their consequences. A decision or choice is a *process* and not an impulsive act. It involves aiming, recruiting, and executing.

We must inspect the aim of our decision, and distinguish whether it is a need or a desire. Needs include shelter, food, and clothing. In meeting needs, we work hard to fortify our ability to love and serve others. In contrast, gratifying desires is more pleasant. But when we choose to gratify desires, we also own the added responsibilities and time attached to fulfilling them. It is selfish to satisfy our desires at the expense of meeting our needs.

Some desires may seem strong; however, if we restrain them, they can weaken and even vanish. On the other hand, internally rehearsed desires gain more strength as they impose themselves on our will, nudging us toward irresponsible decisions.

At one point in my life when I was married with three kids and living in a studio in New Jersey, I wished to go on an exotic vacation. I prayed, and soon enough, I got the news that I would be getting a handsome bonus. I felt grateful, even excited. But as I watched my kids crowding the studio, I realized that God saw my need for a bigger house. Instead of going on a fancy vacation, I used the money for a down payment on my current house.

Once we validate the goal we are targeting, we need to prepare our personal and financial resources, which takes plenty of time. During that time, we should stay connected to dependable friends to receive their encouragement. Their truthfulness also keeps us connected to reality. We need to maximize our preparation and resist the urge to execute our decision quickly.

Noting any deadlines, we carry out our decisions well before they are due. We stay committed to our choice and alter it only when we observe an important change of facts. We remain connected with loved ones, knowing that we experience our self-value through our relationships with them, not through our achievements.

First Corinthians 2:16 says, "For who has known the mind and purposes of the Lord to instruct him but we have the mind of Christ." Having the mind of Christ is an awesome gift, but it is also spiritual in nature. The Holy Spirit reveals the Father's character and attitude. We need to submit to the Holy Spirit to receive His loving, truthful perceptions that displace our carnal and mangled thoughts, transforming our mind into Christ's.

Christians are preoccupied with knowing God's will. But before we know God's will, we need to know God Himself well. Thankfully, He has described His character vividly throughout the Bible. He loves us and longs to have mercy on us.

The Holy Spirit uses His Word, the Bible, to help us think like God, like what He likes, and disapprove of what is displeasing to Him.

I do not know of any book, other than the Bible, which has the power to transform the reader. It comes as no surprise because its Author is alive and present.

Well, we have learned about the contents of the soul. But how do they work together? Do any rules govern their interactions? How can we put that knowledge to use in our fellowship with God and others? Let's find out in the upcoming chapter.

2

Truth in the Innermost Being

My Garden

One hot August day, I was watching the oscillating irrigators as they sprayed water on my landscaping. Some of the water was falling inside the neighbor's garden. I thought to myself, *I hope no one decided to read a book behind the fence.* Getting both yourself and your book suddenly soaked would be quite annoying.

My garden has a cedar wooden pergola with a small herb garden. My neighbor's garden has a stone terrace surrounded by a flawless green lawn and a few short bushes. A fence defines each garden, and each has a unique layout. I can't just barge into the other garden. I need permission from the owner if I want to enter. The other garden is simply not mine.

Had the fence not existed, I would not have distinguished my garden or known the limits for planning decorations or doing projects (like retrieving my daughter's volleyball!).

In the same way that fences define gardens, we have boundaries that define what is ours and what is not. Each one of us owns our own garden. We can't trespass over others' boundaries.

What are the boundaries that define us? Do we practice observing them only when we meet strangers? Should we completely ignore them in romance or marriage? Do we have boundaries with fellow Christians who worship the same God we do? Do we observe boundaries while using social media to interact with others?

What Are Boundaries?

Boundaries are a set of intellectual concepts that define our souls. Despite their existence, the majority of boundaries are intangible. We experience different emotions when others infringe on our boundaries. Here are some examples:

- When a passenger on an airplane invades our space, we feel violated.
- When a social media friend shames our photo, we feel annoyed.
- When a coworker criticizes our beliefs, we feel outraged.

Our soul resembles a garden, and our boundaries are the fences. We are responsible for protecting, caring for, and beautifying our gardens. We don't enter other gardens without their owners' permission, and we are not responsible for other gardens.

So, let's look closer at the boundaries that define us:

1. Body

Our bodies are the physical habitats of our soul, and therefore, we care for and protect them. It may seem that ownership of our bodies is a no-brainer, but we only comprehend ownership of our body after we experience separateness from our parents. If we never experience separateness, we don't perceive our bodies to be part of us. Therefore, our bodies may be assaulted without us perceiving the violation and feeling the grave results at the time. Early violations are experienced when we are mature enough to process their toll.

For example, Julie's innocence was stolen in early childhood, causing her to be relationally delayed. As a teenager, she encountered non-consensual intimate advances from an older boyfriend. Naturally, she does not understand the full implications of the breach against her. Julie needs plenty of love so that she may comprehend her boundaries and form an identity. Only then can she understand her responsibility for protecting her body and saying no to offenders.

2. Time

Time is a valuable boundary. We should use our time to befriend other trustworthy people. Conversely, we should also withhold spending time with those who repeatedly devalue us. We should deprive these repeat offenders of our time and space to restore our safety and let them experience an interruption of our meeting their needs. That may cause them to examine their behavior and take accountability for it.

We need time, truth, and love to grow relationally with others. Therefore, it's wise to use some of our time to befriend others who view us as stable and trustworthy. They love us and give truthful feedback to us. We also need to spend some of our time away from others. This allows us to rest, meditate, and pray; we become more able to clarify our intentions and the intentions of others who want to hurt us, and deal with our emotions.

Individuals who pose a risk to us relationally do not respect our ownership of our time or our way of using it. Here's an example:

Michael felt angry with Samantha at a wedding party. He accused her of flirting with other guys and then insulted her. Samantha was hurt and saddened by his words. She cared for Michael, but she understood the seriousness of his offense.

She quietly left and stayed with other friends for a while. She spent a few days leaning on her friends for empathy and encouragement. Michael called the next day, but she responded to his call with a message requesting that he respect her and therefore declined to spend time with him.

In the time spent alone, Michael began to comprehend the

harm he had inflicted on Samantha with his harsh words. He reached out to an old church friend, who invited him to seek accountability and help.

3. Place

Our place represents the physical room around us. Each one of us has an emotionally safe place. It could be the kitchen for a household person, the bedroom for a teenager, or the office for someone who works from home.

When we succeed in separating from our caregivers, we form our identity and relate to others as distinct. In relating through the distinctness lens, we respect the safe places of others and request their permission for us to enter. When we are level with others, we refrain from criticizing their places, no matter how humble they are.

I was visiting a friend who works as a chemist. He wanted to show me his home. We toured various rooms and eventually stopped at a small dark room, where he explained that its purpose was to farm worms. I showed interest and asked him to tell me more. His eyes brightened, and he went on a mini verbal marathon, explaining the benefits of raising worms and how to feed them. I genuinely thanked him for sharing. I told him that visiting the worm room helped me get to know him better. He nodded in agreement.

When we choose a place to manage conflicts with others, however, we need to negotiate a place that is emotionally neutral for both parties. It is offensive for us to enter someone's safe place and insist on settling a conflict.

We shouldn't give others access to our safe place until we have built trust with them. If we experience threats while at a certain place, we should relocate ourselves to a safe location.

4. Words of expression and protection

When we use words that express our views, beliefs, and emotions, we help others recognize our intellectual and emotional boundaries so they can honor them. The love motive directs us to speak our truthful emotional response. We need to first honor others before giving them our feedback. Giving honor first fortifies listeners so they can withstand our truthfulness.

In divulging our attitudes, memories, and feelings, we perform "self-disclosure"—the cornerstone of exchanging love and seeking healing. However, we need to build trust with others before we begin disclosing ourselves, and the disclosure is done gradually, gently, and mutually.

We need to express our needs and desires to our relational partners so that, in turn, they will collaborate with us to examine and provide for them. Conversely, when we sulk, we devalue our partners by giving them the impossible mission of scanning our minds and reading our thoughts. This inevitably leads to frustration, confusion, and strife.

When we split between good and bad, we hide our flaws and shortcomings. The hiding resembles wearing a mask. Being a physician, I experienced people's displeasure with masks during the Covid pandemic. Masks seemed to make breathing harder. Similarly, wearing an intellectual mask drains our energy and erodes our freedom to be authentic.

We need to use the proper words to protect ourselves from harm and violations. Saying *no* constitutes our most important protective word. For example, we can say,

- "I want no part of this TikTok prank; it is dangerous."
- "I refuse your sarcastic jokes."
- "I don't appreciate comments about my body shape."
- "I don't agree with you on vilifying the officer who gave you a ticket for speeding!"

During separateness, we start saying the word *no* to differentiate ourselves and affirm ownership. We learn to use *no* properly when our caregivers continue to love and protect us. Our ability to respond with *no* to offense represents our protective emotional muscle. If we experience the withdrawal of love in response to using it, we tend to avoid using it and instead, use a false *yes*. This is how compliance is born.

When we form an identity, we use "I" to express ourselves. Others who lack identities use "we" to define themselves. They avoid expressing personal thoughts, filling their speech with gossip and rumors.

5. Trustworthy friends

We want people, not things, to be our best friends. In making friendships, we grow in our ability to build trust and disclose ourselves. We lean on friends for listening to us and giving empathy when we experience violation. We recruit encouragement and power from them to take a stand against offenders and deploy consequences. As we request and accept their help, we learn humility and patience.

If I sit in my decade-old Volvo truck, I notice that behind it and along its sides, there are blind spots that I can't see. (Newer models are equipped with cameras to detect objects in their blind spots.) Relationships have similar emotional blind spots that we cannot detect. Our friends' truthful feedback illuminates the blind spots and gets us closer to reality. We need humility to accept their truthful statements.

It is risky to pursue romantic love without the safety of being connected in deep friendships. Romantic connections are deep, and when they are severed, they trigger pain and sadness. Our relational isolation would make the pain more agonizing. If romance were flying, friendship would be the parachute.

6. Consequences

When we are secure in our identities, we understand we must take responsibility for our choices. We learn patience, delayed gratification, and empathy when we bear the consequences of our decisions. While an apology conveys kindness, owning responsibility conveys love.

The love motive guides us to deploy constructive consequences toward repeat offenders. One powerful consequence is removing ourselves from their company. Removing ourselves serves two purposes: it guards our hearts and lets offenders comprehend how our presence nurtured them in the past. Before we become capable of removing ourselves, we need to have deepened friendships with trustworthy people, so we can lean on their love and encouragement.

We should deploy consequences toward offenders kindly and responsibly. Our motive is to help them experience ownership of responsibility. We do not aim to punish or harm. For example, after the first offense, we refuse the violation and ask for respect for our boundaries. After their second offense, we affirm our refusal and express the intention to deploy consequences on them. We may offer offenders alternatives at this stage. If the violation continues, we tell them we will deploy consequences without further warnings. Once again, being in other friendship relationships allows us to recruit the power needed to use consequences on the offender.

A heavy drinker, Mike returned home late one night. He woke up his wife, Sarah, to fix him dinner. She complied to keep the peace. Mike started ranting about her silence and cursed her.

Sarah had previously voiced refusal of his abuse. In the past, she and several church friends had pleaded with Mike to attend rehab. When Mike threw a plate at her on this night, she dodged it before she ran to the bedroom, locked the door, and called the police.

Officers removed Mike from the house, and the court ordered him to stay away from her. He was to attend rehabilitation and behavioral therapy. He was also placed on temporary suspension from his job. In the aftermath, Mike realized how selfish and harmful his behavior was.

Meanwhile, Sarah met with a small group in her church to get support and encouragement. She expressed that she intended to prioritize her safety and let Mike face responsibility for his actions.

Jesus said in John 10:10, "The thief comes only to steal, kill and destroy. I came that you may have life and have it in abundance."

Jesus intended life to be abundant. I believe an abundant emotional life starts from within us. On the other side, Jesus desires to be in a personal relationship with us. Thus, it is urgent that we define ourselves so He can relate to us.

When we define ourselves, we become better equipped to receive Jesus personally. We discern His holy thoughts and enjoy His embrace. We claim our position in Him and receive His covenants as personal promises. He becomes no longer just God, He becomes Abba.

So what are the contents within the self? How do they interact with each other? Let's find out in the next chapter on how wonderfully we are made.

3

Know the Laws

Traffic Across Boundaries

Listening to classical music after a busy day, I watched the automated screensaver displayed on my television. It depicted airplanes taxiing on runways at a crowded airport. The planes looked like miniature toys as they navigated an elaborate labyrinth of intersections and roundabouts. I thought about how air traffic controllers have their work cut out for them. They rely on rules to speed up the movements of airplanes, even if it's just taxiing! At the same time, they prioritize safety.

The traffic of emotions, information, and thoughts across our boundaries resembles airport traffic. Our will resembles an air traffic controller. Guided by our motives, it either permits or rejects the flow. In doing so, it must observe specific rules to stay safe while giving and receiving love.

Rules of Opening and Closing

So, let's find out about those rules that regulate the opening and closing of our boundaries.

1. Motive matters

God examines the motives behind our relationships. "All a person's ways seem pure to them, but motives are weighed by the Lord" (Proverbs 16:2). The most important motive behind opening or closing ourselves to others is giving and receiving love.

God tells us in Scripture that He desires us to be rooted in love:

So that Christ may dwell in your hearts through faith. And I pray that you, being rooted and established in love, may have power, together with all the Lord's holy people, to grasp how side and long and high and deep is the love of Christ (Ephesians 3:16-18).

Becoming rooted in love will help us disclose our injuries to trustworthy recipients so we can receive their empathy and truthful feedback. In contrast, when we live under fear, we play the victim. It is empathy and truth that help us modify our current perceptions of our old injuries and therefore feel better and healed.

If fortune favors the brave, then love favors the trustworthy! We need to open our boundaries to them to give and receive love. You may wonder, *Didn't Jesus command us to love our enemies in Matthew 5:44?* He did, but He didn't ask us to open ourselves to them and have a relationship with them.

We can honor and speak truth to those who offend us, but we need to guard our heart from their abandonment, betrayal, and rejection. On the other hand, when someone violates us, we should secure our boundaries—our time, place, or thoughts—against them. We halt sharing with them. Our motive behind closing our boundaries is to protect our soul's ability to give and receive love with others.

When offenders come up against our newly sealed boundaries, they may recognize how our presence until now was nurturing their needs. That recognition, as painful as it is, offers offenders an opportunity to take more responsibility for their words and actions. Offenders have free will, and they may react with anger and withdrawal. In this case, we can search for relationships with others who are more loving and responsible.

At times, however, we may close or open our boundaries because we are driven by the wrong motive. Here are some examples:

- We open our boundaries to irresponsible people due to our fear of loneliness.
- We open our boundaries to manipulative people who lure us with false responsibility.
- We close our boundaries to worthy people due to apathy, or worse, to inflict harm on them.
- We close our boundaries to trustworthy people due to our false need to please close family members.

We aim to know others' truthful feedback through listening, not assuming. Through *the distinctness lens*, we comprehend that others are responsible for expressing their needs and desires. On our end, we are responsible for hearing our partners, examining their wants, and providing for some of them.

When we choose to sulk instead of expressing ourselves, we push the responsibility of expressing our wants onto others. In doing this, we leave our partners in the darkness of assumption. Consider this real-life example:

It is Christopher's birthday. His wife, Michelle, returns home after a long day's work. She greets him but then immediately senses coldness in his tone of voice and notices that he is avoiding eye contact with her.

Christopher takes a few bites of his food and then quietly withdraws to the bedroom. Feeling frustrated, Michelle tells him to just say what he wants from her. He replies with resentment, "You know too well what I want!"

If Christopher had expressed his desire to be celebrated, his loving spouse would have provided him with celebration. But instead, he refused to voice his thoughts, and coldness prevailed. Refusal to express ourselves spurs frustration, misunderstanding, and conflict.

2. Respect is mutual

Through the *levelness lens, we perceive others as equal to us.* We honor their boundaries and want them to honor ours. We especially want to respect when other people say no. If others refuse our requests, we must continue to treasure them despite our disappointment. It is helpful to have several friendships so that we can diversify meeting our needs among them. This way, if a friend declines our request, we can submit the request to another friend. It is challenging for a single relationship to serve as our lone emotional support because it will stagger under all the emotional needs.

When we reconcile the good and bad within ourselves, we relate through the integration lens. We comprehend that when others refuse our requests, they don't reject us as individuals. Those who relate through the splitting lens can't make such a distinction. They perceive the refusal of their request as a rejection, and feel hurt and shunned. In reality, the refusal of requests is normal, even necessary, in love relationships.

We want to rein in our disappointment when others refuse our requests. We focus on comprehending how the refusal of others helps them guard their heart and soul. We may find our requests to be irresponsible, selfish, or impulsive. The refusal of our requests can lead us to grow in responsibility and overcome selfishness. Here is an example:

Ian sees an advertisement for an electric bicycle and pictures himself riding it to work. He asks his wife to apply for a line of credit loan to help him buy it. The mature wife affirms her love for him and declines. She wants to save money for the next IVF cycle. Ian initially feels disappointed, but after talking to his church buddy, he recognizes that his request was rash and somewhat selfish.

3. Jurisdiction is within

In forming an identity and relating through the *distinctness lens, we comprehend that the jurisdiction of our power is limited to within ourselves.* God's divine power gave us all we need for a godly life (2 Peter 1:3). When we submit to the Holy Spirit, we can effectively change what is inside us.

We can apply this power to challenge our distorted thoughts and grow in responsibility. That is what repentance looks like. Repentance almost always produces growth and invites others to follow our path.

While we don't want to use our power to engage in vengeance and strife, we can use it to remove ourselves from the presence of offenders. It is one of the most powerful consequences we can deploy in response to repeated offenses.

God empowers us to request help in situations marked by an increase in legitimate needs. These include those for shelter, food, clothing, or health. In petitioning friends for help, we overcome pride and impatience. Through the distinctness lens, we open some of our boundaries to allow help to get in, while we maintain ownership of our remaining boundaries.

God's power manifests in His love. We can harness His love to forgive others. Receiving His loving perceptions enables us to resume loving offenders and confessing their freedom and equality. We will need to renounce our demands for justice.

Forgiveness reveals our dire need for being grounded in God's love. It requires an outpouring of *agape* love that transcends our human inclination. We can't resume loving others who have offended us without first receiving Jesus' love and reflecting on His forgiveness for the ones who offended Him.

Since our power is incapable, even illegitimate, inside others' jurisdictions, we need to petition God to work inside their boundaries. The exception would be the case in which others petition us to enter their boundaries during help-worthy situations.

4. Accepting hurt and refusing harm

We need to distinguish between emotional hurt and harm. Hurt is a feeling of distress, anguish, and suffering. We feel hurt when we perceive offense, loss, and owning additional responsibilities. Feeling hurt is uncomfortable, but the feeling shines light on our perceptions, responsibilities, and demands. Despite feeling hurt, we preserve both our identity and the perception of being valued. These are a few examples of hurts:

- We feel hurt when offended.

- We hurt when we let go of our distorted thoughts after receiving truthfulness (as in healing). Solomon writes in Proverbs 27:6, "Wounds from a friend can be trusted, but an enemy multiplies kisses."

- We feel pain when we give up our demands (worthy or not).

- We feel pain when we own additional responsibility (as forgiveness).

On the other hand, harm mutilates identity and degrades self-value. We experience harm when others target our identity and reduce our worth. Paradoxically the feeling of pain may not be present during an occurance of harm.

If our first encounter with hurt came in the form of harm, we assume that harm and hurt are identical. This is likely to happen in abuse and neglect. We react by avoiding hurt at any price and opting for withdrawal, which is ironically harmful! A life that is centered around avoiding pain is selfish and devoid of love and truthfulness. David accepted hurt as the way to learn God's precepts. Psalm 119:17 says, "It was good for me to be afflicted so that I might learn your decrees."

God is love. First John 4:7 says, "Let us love one another, for love comes from God. Everyone who loves has been born of God and knows God." He doesn't harm us, but His righteousness can be perceived as hurtful. This is due to our fallen nature. David affirmed his trust in God's kindness even when he was hurt. Psalms 119:75-76 says, "I know, Lord, that your laws are righteous, and that in faithfulness you have afflicted me. May your unfailing love be my comfort according to your promise to your servant."

In a similar manner, we want to value those who relate through the devaluation lens before deploying consequences against them. We affirm their value as we invite them to responsibility. We may even help them if they experience harm during ownership.

5. Zeroing the counter

Jesus says in Luke 6:45 (NKJV), "For out of the abundance [overflow] of the heart his mouth speaks." The message is clear: what we store in our hearts will come out as words.

If we were harmed before becoming conscious of self, we don't perceive the injury, nor do we process its emotional toll. Later in life, when we resume our relational growth, we take the first inventory of our emotional stores. We glance at our emotional counter and note high levels of fear, anger, shame, and sadness.

In becoming conscious of our emotional baggage, we experience a tsunami of negative emotions. Left unchecked, the flood overwhelms our will and ignites cutting words and impulsive actions. We need to restore our emotional balance, which is zeroing the counter.

We zero the counter by verbalizing our stored emotions to concerned listeners and receive their grace, empathy, and truth. Verbalizing can be draining, but it is a temporary process. It is the bridge from the old self that reacts to the new self that responds.

Notably, we need to inspect our demands and abolish the unworthy ones. Letting go of demands is painful, even when the demands are undoable. We no longer resort to destructive anger to defend ourselves from looming violations. We recognize that our deliberate choices, not explosive reactions, are the best protection. We speak better words out of our heart, and better yet, can command our speech inflections.for, after all, it is not just *what* we speak, but *how* we speak it.

God's motive behind disclosing Himself is love. At the same time, He respects our free will and does not force His disclosure on us. I have always wondered how God did disclose Himself uninvited to Paul on the road to Damascus, as described in Acts 9:1.

Saul was a staunch Pharisee who thought he was serving God by persecuting the new wave of blasphemers. In Acts 7, He witnessed Stephen asking his God to forgive those who were stoning him. Saul must have been deeply moved by what he witnessed, as he invited this "forgiving God" to reveal Himself. Shortly after, this forgiving God disclosed kindly in Act 9:5, "I am Jesus, whom you are persecuting."

Like Paul, you may think you know God, but it pays to invite this forgiving God to reveal Himself to you. Paul's life changed because he did, and yours would too!

When we open and close ourselves according to the relational laws, we reap amazing fruits in our lives. Let us find out more about those fruits.

4

Wheat Not Thistles

Reaping

I started my car and hit the road—the garden state parkway—to visit my therapist. Feeling excited, I reflected on what I would share. I had gone through weeks of hurt and sadness, but I learned to deal with it by leaning on God's love and His promises. My fellow saints offered love, grace, and truth, which helped me claim my boundaries and define my identity. Upon arriving at my appointment, I expressed my thoughts and feelings with a good pace and infectious energy.

I shared how much I had tried to rescue others from their irresponsible choices, trying to "pay" for love. I reflected on how I broke free from false responsibility and felt freer and more able.

The session ended with my therapist applauding my progress in challenging my biggest illusion. He reminded me to stay connected with trustworthy friends. He added that I could see him less often, which was good for me and my checkbook! Sessions are not cheap, but if you ask me, they are worth every penny.

I had a remarkable turnaround. I finally experienced rest and freedom. I routinely expressed my thoughts, comforting others with the grace that had comforted me. Better yet, having defined myself, I internalized my spiritual position as an overcomer in Him. When we open ourselves to trustworthy others and close ourselves against irresponsible and harmful boundaries, we grow in personal responsibility and freedom.

Responsibility

When we think about our boundaries, we can clearly distinguish the lines of our responsibility. Personal responsibility is significant but also limited. It is a lot less than what we tend to assume before forming a distinct identity.

1. The personal responsibility for self

When we affirm boundaries, we begin ownership of our thoughts. The Holy Spirit dwells in us, but He doesn't coerce us. When we submit to Him willfully, we replace selfish illusions with love and truthfulness.

By defining our identity and accepting His lordship, we begin modeling our identity in the light of our spiritual position in God. We are alive with Him (Ephesians 2:5), complete in Him (Colossians 2:10), holy (1 Peter 1:16), doers of His Word (James 1:22), free from the law of sin and death (Romans 8:2), and joint-heirs with Christ (Romans 8:17). Claiming God's covenants as personal promises guides and transforms us into responsible servants.

We are responsible for enriching our thoughts. For every false perception we renounce, we make room to receive a new truthful one. We need to receive love and honest perceptions to form the distinctness lens. Through it, we can honor others' freedom and refuse any false responsibility.

We need to accept personal responsibility for our erratic emotional responses. We must overcome fear and seek wholehearted listeners for understanding and truthful feedback. We embrace the hurt of writing off emotional debts.

We are responsible for distinguishing our worthy demands for hearing, understanding, and equality. We grow in patience and long-suffering in canceling unworthy or unjust demands. As a result we want to liberate others from the false responsibility of meeting all our needs.

Our responsibility consists of ownership of choices. We note that procrastination and compliance constitute choices too. We need to ask for help if experiencing the consequences of our choices harm us.

We may think that we own our bodies, but in reality, they are leased to us by our loving Creator. They are containers of His glory, and He needs them to advance His kingdom's work. We want to take good care of our earthly tents. As we seal ourselves against irresponsible others, we free more time and resources for health, rest, and good nutrition.

God helps with our excessively heavy needs. "Praise be to the Lord, to God our Savior, who daily bears our burdens" (Psalm 68:19). On the other hand, Paul sets a fantastic example of owning personal responsibility in his letter to the Thessalonian church: "Surely you remember, brothers and sisters, our toil and hardship; we worked night and day not to be a burden to anyone while we preached the gospel of God to you" (1 Thessalonians 2:9).

2. Responsibility toward others

The love motive guides us to do the best for others. When we relate through the *distinctness lens*, we recognize that others are separate from us, and therefore, responsible for what exists within their own boundaries. If we were to assume their responsibilities, we would rob them of their opportunities to grow.

Persuading people who are irresponsible is futile. They learn responsibility only through the pain of consequences. Emotional consequences are *experienced* more than logically *explained*. "A man of great anger, will bear the penalty; for if you rescue him, you will only have to save him over and over again" (Proverbs 19:19 AMP). We want to declare that we treasure others before clarifying our intentions to them of declining to bear their responsibilities.

We sympathize with others who feel hurt due to their newly owned responsibilities. Nonetheless, most of their hurt results from their distorted perceptions. They may even accuse us of selfishness or cruelty. Contrary to such accusations, refusing false responsibility increases our ability to obey the love motive and serve those in need.

Responsibility for self doesn't entirely rule out helping others harmed by the consequences of their decisions. Love doesn't practice indifference in the face of harm. In the help-worthy scenario, we need to help and call on others to help.

The Scripture instructs help during the harmful times: "Do not forsake your friend or a friend of your family, and do not go to your relative's house when disaster strikes you—better a neighbor nearby than a relative far away" (Proverbs 27:10).

It may not be straightforward to distinguish between the help-worthy situation and the unworthy one, and one can morph into the other. We want to listen wholeheartedly to those requesting help for us to dispense understanding and empathy. We remain connected also with our trustworthy friends to get their perceptions of the situation and better appreciate it. In helping others, we aim to build momentum for them to resume ownership of their responsibilities.

Finally, how we furnish help is as vital as our decision to help. We need to preserve the worth of those being helped and cross only the relevant boundaries necessary for delivering help. We safeguard their privacy, especially on social media. It is devaluing to help others and, in the process, scatter their details in front of everyone.

Freedom

Freedom goes hand in hand with responsibility. As we take

ownership of our emotional content, such as fear, guilt, and envy, we grow in freedom. We are never free without being responsible. Conversely, we are responsible for what we do in freedom.

1. Freedom from fear

In experiencing separateness from others, we recognize that offenders are powerless inside our boundaries. We can overcome the fear they use to intimidate us. They can't violate us unless we open ourselves and let them in. We can deploy consequences if they force their way in despite our refusal.

We need to be in relationships that help us become perfected in love. This way, we won't be tempted to open our boundaries to risky relational others because of fear. "There is no fear in love. But perfect love drives out fear, because fear has to do with punishment. The one who fears is not made perfect in love" (1 John 4:18).

We can be free from manipulators who used to push our buttons. We tighten our time and seal our place against them (including on social media). We respond and no longer react. We name our emotions, identify the triggering word or actions, and verbalize the feelings to wholehearted listeners.

2. Freedom from guilt

In becoming distinct, we can treasure others without setting qualifiers. This, in turn, frees the receivers from paying us back and allows them to experience gratitude. They can reciprocate in love should they choose to. The love cycle consists of love, gratitude, then loving back. Acts of honor that insist on your meeting qualifiers before they are done are manipulative and induce guilt, not gratitude from you. "Let each one give as he has made up his own mind and purposed in his heart, not reluctantly or sorrowfully or under compulsion, for God loves a cheerful giver" (2

Corinthians 9:7).

We need to receive only unconditional love from others in order to be free to experience gratitude. On the other hand, by our accepting conditional love acts, we co-sign the debt for the payback. Thanksgiving is therefore liberating because it frees us from compulsively paying back for love.

Scripture tells us to give thanks in all situations: "Give thanks in all circumstances for this is God's will for you in Christ Jesus" (1 Thessalonians 5:18). We are grateful not for the difficult situations but for God's unconditional love that cushions us during these challenges.

3. Freedom from envy

When we form a distinct identity, we begin the exciting search for treasure buried inside our boundaries. We need the Holy Spirit's enlightenment and the counsel of trustworthy saints to unearth our talents. Life gets abundant when we embark on growing our discovered skills.

If we don't invest our time in unearthing and growing our talents, we succumb to envy. We shift our focus to desiring what others have and wishing to live someone else's life. It is a false hope that leads to despair and resentment. We need to translate Solomon's warning in Proverbs 24:19 "not to be envious of the wicked" as a wake-up call to enrich our righteous life.

Rather than envying others and wishing to be them, we should embrace our identity by celebrating our skills and harnessing the power to face our flaws and become unique. Love creates the authentic, while fear perverts. Looking at Jesus, the author and finisher of our faith, we see that He has a rock-solid identity. His life manifested freedom and responsibility.

In Matthew 23:37, Jesus said, "O Jerusalem, Jerusalem, you who kill the prophets and stone those sent to you, how often I have longed to gather your children together, as a hen gathers her chicks under her wings, and you were not willing." Jesus expressed His desire to connect with Jerusalem's people, but at the same time, He respected their freedom. He is free and therefore honors others' freedom.

"So let us seize and hold fast and retain without wavering the hope we cherish and confess and our acknowledgement of it, for He Who promised is reliable and faithful to His word" (Hebrews 10:23 AMPC).

Jesus reliably owned the responsibility of saving us. He spent years patiently getting ready. When His time of service came, He traveled to meet the hungry and hurt. He went to synagogues to preach and heal. Jesus accepted the responsibility of saving us, knowing it would cost Him dearly. He willingly submitted to the cross.

Let's work on building our identity and growing in responsibility. We have an advocate for power and counsel in the Holy Spirit.

5

Emotions Shed the Light

Feeling Them All

My phone vibrated and slid toward the edge of the nightstand table. I ignored the vibrations, initially in hopes of getting more sleep, but upon seeing the sunshine beam across the windows, I picked it up. A family member had posted about the death of my beloved aunt on social media. My eyes welled with tears as my mind replayed childhood memories of her bandaging my scraped knees.

Finishing my solitary prayer time, I geared up for the big day. My daughter was going to the National Spelling Bee. A wave of joy swept over me as I reflected on her achievement.

As we were commuting to the conference hotel, I received a phone call from my hospital's lawyer. He asked to schedule a meeting concerning the upcoming lawsuit trial. I felt momentary apprehension, but I reassured myself, muttering, "I can do all things in you, Lord." Part of me silently screamed in frustration, *Why do lawyers request essential things at 5 p.m. on a Friday?*

The day reminds me of paddleboarding on a windy day. Just as the waves of a lake push and pull against a board, divergent emotions push and pull daily. We want to distinguish our feelings and the perceptions that trigger them. Our higher aim is to renew our distorted perceptions and relate through sound lenses.

So, let's find out more about the primary emotions: fear, sadness, anger, and joy.

1. Sadness

Sadness is a low mood. When we feel sad, we sob and weep. We become slow in our thoughts and words. We feel sadness when we experience loss or disappointment in hopes. We may withdraw from others to conserve our energy. A few people may even become falsely cheerful when about to experience sadness.

When we relate to others, we form emotional ties with them. If we lose the relationship, we experience the tear of the emotional ties. That, in turn, triggers feelings of sadness, hurt, and longing. The Apostle described in 1 Thessalonians 2:17 how they felt orphaned in separation. We feel sadness, maybe to a lesser extent, after losing social media connections.

We certainly need to refrain from starting random relationships. We want to seek God and the counsel of our trustworthy friends before pursuing relationships and sharing ourselves.

When we don't bond with loved ones, we regress to making connections with material belongings. If we were to lose those belongings, we would grieve them intensely.

We grieve over lost pets. Pets provide us with physical touches, companionship, and loyalty. We should recognize the magnitude of grief for pet owners who are not grounded in deep friendships.

Sadness or any felt emotion can be genuinely appreciated by those who experience it. We need to grow in our ability to grieve with others. We do it by learning to be present with them without preaching, reasoning, or cheering them on.

We also feel sadness when we experience the failure of our immature hopes. We begin learning how to hope in early childhood. We hope immaturely that achievements, prosperity, or fame will get us loved. When those false hopes fail to bring us love and value, we experience disappointment and despair.

In contrast, when we mature in hope, we see in close relationships the path to living in self-value. We accept reality, relinquish selfishness, and relate with others, motivated by love.

In embracing grief, we treat sadness. But by abandoning false hopes, we protect ourselves from despair. We became adept at hiding our genuine fragility behind the virtual facade of social media. Therefore, I think it may be better to assume that others are emotionally fragile until proven otherwise.

Let's distinguish between ordinary sadness and depression. We feel ordinary sadness for less than two weeks. We remain able to think clearly and enjoy ourselves. We stay related to others and can sleep, eat, and have intimacy.

In contrast, in depression, we experience a static state of sadness that persists for longer than two weeks—perhaps months or years. We slow our thought processing to ease the pain of conflicting perceptions. We struggle with eating, sleeping, and working.

It is somewhat arrogant to expect that we would be able to help ourselves out of depression. When we cease to relate to others and God, sadness can block us from seeing any exits. People who are depressed may consider terminating life as their only way out.

God feels sadness. Isaiah 53:3 says, "He is despised and rejected by men, a man of sorrow and pain and acquainted with grief; and like one from home man hide their faces he was despised, and we did not appreciate his worth or esteem him." God grieves when we sin, as when we reject His lordship or trespass with others. We tend to underestimate how vulnerable God is. We hurt Him often, but He patiently embraces us.

2. Fear

Emotions are personal, but fear is more uniquely so. For most of us, we experience fear as tightness and an expectation of doom. For a few daredevils, however, fear is excitement. During fear, our heart races, our eyes widen, and our chin retracts.

We feel fear when we encounter a threat. A threat can be factual, like that of a physical injury, but most threats are perceived when we examine an interaction we've had with someone and interpret it as threatening. The latter case stems from the attitude we use to approach the event. Our relational attitude or lens dictates how we relate to others and how to decipher their interaction.

For example, a policeman stops a driver for a traffic violation. When the driver reaches for his phone, the policeman perceives a threat and sternly tells him to keep his hands where he can see them.

We feel fear when we perceive the possibility of losing love, potential rejection, condemnation, or ridicule. We may also fear losing privacy or falling short on a task. We need to acknowledge the feelings of fear and persist in holding tight to the love motive. The Apostle Paul felt fear approaching the Corinthian but went anyway with the power of the Holy Spirit. "I came to you in weakness with great fear and trembling" (1 Corinthians 2:3).

Scripture diagnoses fear as being not perfected in love: "There is no fear in love, but perfect love casts out fear because fear has to do with punishment. The one who fears is not made perfect in love" (1 John 4:18). When we do not receive enough love to feel secure, we adopt fear as a motive and approach others through the devaluation lens.

Through the *devaluation lens, we value things more than people*. We do not have a loving, responsible way to meet our needs. We invade others' time or space to get what we want. We intimidate others with death stares, verbal insults, or even physical or sexual violence toward them. We may devalue others covertly by luring them out of their boundaries to use them and discard them after getting what we want.

Solomon warns about fearing others, calling it a trap: "Fear of man will prove to be a snare, but whoever trusts in the Lord is kept safe" (Proverbs 29:25).

3. Anger

Anger is the energy we produce to meet our demands. Frank anger manifests in visible signs like frowning, high inflection, and tight body posture. Subtle anger manifests in sarcasm, passive-aggressive behavior, and deliberate procrastination. We may feel anger to shield ourselves from the realization of unbearable perceptions like fearing the loss of love.

God doesn't use anger to destroy. In Hosea 11:9, He says, "I will not carry out my fierce anger, nor will I devastate Ephraim again. I am God, not a man—the Holy One among you. I will not come against their cities."

As we form an identity, we relate through the distinctness lens. We become conscious that emotions are only part of the soul. We begin to take ownership of our emotions. We learn to contain our anger and constructively harness it to correct unjust or irresponsible behavior. We also stop perceiving anger as a personal attack. In Matthew 21:12, Jesus expressed constructive anger as He demanded His Father's home be set apart for worship, not trade: "He overturned the tables of the money changers and the benches of those selling doves." Jesus didn't degrade traders but gave His truthful feedback about what they were doing.

When we relate through *the compliance lens*, we store a trough of passive anger. We carefully choose sarcastic comments to needle others. We destroy their special occasions by being purposely late. We may give them the silent treatment and cease communicating with them in any shape or form.

When we relate through *the levelness lens*, we extend equal respect to others' demands. But through *the disparity lens*, we perceive others as beneath us and dismiss their demands. I was with some colleagues on a social outing one day. I voiced my dislike about vaccine mandates. I said, "I oppose mandates and prefer dialogue to engage parents in the decision." An older colleague, who is a staunch supporter of mandates, became infuriated. His anger reflected his unjust demands because I was equal and entitled to a different opinion.

All our demands seem just to us. But Proverbs 14:12 gives the sober reminder that "there is a way which seems right to a man and appears straight before him, but at the end of it, it's the way of death." We need the truthfulness of our trustworthy saints to sift through our demands and pick up the worthy ones such as equality, hearing, and respect. At the same time, we need to forfeit the unworthy ones, even if they feel fair.

Canceling demands, just or unjust, is going to hurt. Author Joyce Meyer calls this a flesh burner. We need to ask for grace and surrender to the Great Potter so He can gently mold us. We need to resist withdrawal and grumbling. We are comforted knowing that when our flesh is wasted, our inner man is reshaped to be like Him: "Therefore, we don't lose heart. Though outwardly we are wasting away, yet inwardly we are being renewed day by day" (2 Corinthians 4:16).

4. Joy

We feel joy when we experience provision, achievement, and health. We express this joy through laughter, cheerful expressions, and relaxed body postures.

Joy is inseparable from the relationships we engage in. The joy of being accepted, understood, and treasured is only possible within relationships with trusted people.

God enjoys our fellowship more than our service. Therefore,

we must nurture intimacy with Him and shed the guilt of meeting everyone's needs. As we abide in Him, we learn to serve guided by His loving Spirit, not the relentless worldly push.

Joy is a burst, while *contentment is a state that comes from aligning our priorities with God's callings.* Contentment keeps us anchored to God's love as we ride life's roller coasters. This is what the apostle Paul told the Philippine church. "I am not saying this because I am in need, for I have learned to be content whatever the circumstances" (Philippians 4:11). In contentment, we are fulfilled inside and less reliant on outcomes to be happy. We give thanks in our noisy neighborhood, long waiting lines, or cloudy days, for example.

We read in Luke 10:21 (AMP) what makes Jesus feel joy: "I praise you, O Father, Lord of heaven and earth, that You have hidden these things from the wise and intelligent and have revealed them to infants." Jesus is joyful as He experienced His Father's salvation plan, understood and treasured by the disciples.

God said that everything He created was good. He created emotions to help us inspect our perceived threats, demands, and losses.

Those perceptions, in turn, form our relational lenses. The formation has orderly stages. It is an exciting order I can't wait to share with you.

6

Wonderfully Made

Relational by Design

My cordless work phone rang with a call from a nervous nurse. She told me tensely that they needed a neonatologist for an emergency in room 13. I squeezed the mask over my nose to prevent fogging and grabbed my newborn-sized stethoscope. Walking briskly toward the labor room, I wondered, with a hint of frustration, *Where did the emergency come from?* The charge nurse had told me during the morning huddle that we were expecting only normal deliveries.

The labor nurse greeted me and told me that a pregnant mom came into early labor and was expected to give birth to a thirty-week premature baby. I countered my surging apprehension by taking a few deep breaths and checking the resuscitation equipment. The clock ticked for a few minutes. Silence gave way to push instructions, followed by screams and cheerful applause! The baby was born!

As soon as the newborn was handed to me, I dried her off and cleaned her up. Doing my routine assessment, I estimated that she weighed six to seven pounds. She was closer to a term baby than premature. Feeling relieved, I congratulated the parents and asked the nurse to assist the mother in bonding with her newborn.

We can estimate physical growth and development because established norms help the assessment. Because the baby's weight in this scenario was not outside the norm for newborns, she was deemed to be mature. However, it isn't easy to estimate someone's relational growth without knowing the typical milestones. Some of us aren't even sure that such norms exist. I would argue that many people lack insight into their stage of relational growth.

Our physical development consists of sequential stages. A new stage is marked by skills that are built on the former ones. We learn how to stand before we walk. Our relational growth resembles the physical one because it also consists of stages.

The way we perceive others produces how we feel about them—we produce emotions in response to perceiving. We rely on formed perceptions to infer threats, demands, or losses within our relationships. It is easy to understand why. Relational situations are not clear-cut, logical facts. Two people can perceive the same relational event quite differently. We can trace what we feel back to our way of relating. Relational events are the key triggers for emotions.

The Psalmist concluded that some of our harm is due to our distorted ways: "Some are fools because of their transgressions and are afflicted because of their iniquities" (Psalm107:17). In Psalm 19:3, David explains how foolish perceptions will thwart our way of doing things: "The foolishness of man subverts his way [ruins his affairs]; then his heart is resentful and frets against the Lord." Ironically, we take our frustration and anger on God instead of taking responsibility for our faulty ways of interacting.

God the Father is permanently and eternally related in love to Jesus and the Holy Spirit: "Believe Me when I say that I am in the Father and the Father is in Me" (John 14:11). Jesus often and always thanked the Father for His love, while the Holy Spirit, who came from the Father, told the truth about Jesus, the King: "I will ask the Father, and he will give you another advocate to help you and be with you forever—the Spirit of truth. The world cannot accept him, because it neither sees him nor knows him. But you know him, for he lives with you and will be in you" (John 14:16-17). The Scripture depicts God's relational nature. We observe in the Old Testament that God's principles address relationships among others and between them and God Himself. As for the New Testament, we observe Jesus, our beloved Savior, relating to His disciples as friends: "I no longer call you servants, because a servant does not know his master's business. Instead, I have called you friends, for everything that I learned from my Father I have made known to you" (John 15:15).

Jesus often taught love, faith, and hope through parables about people in relationships. The Apostle Paul observed how the Thessalonians grew simultaneously in love and faith: "We ought always to thank God for you, brothers and sisters, and rightly so, because your faith is growing more and more, and the love all of you have for one another is increasing" (2 Thessalonians 1:3).

David praised God in Psalm 139:14:"I praise you because I am fearfully and wonderfully made; your works are wonderful, I know that full well." God made us wonderfully in His image (Genesis 1:27). We are relational like Him too. Hallelujah!

Throughout early life, we register people's interactions around us as perceptions of how things should or shouldn't be. We use these relational perceptions over time to construct our own relational attitude or relational lenses. We constantly use our relational lenses to approach others and seek our needs and wants to be fulfilled. We also use them to manage conflicts, relate to authority, and more importantly, to God.

Stages and Lenses

Relational growth, like physical growth, has stages. When

41

we accomplish a particular stage, we can relate through a specific relational lens and perform relational milestones. Growing into advanced stages results from growth during former stages. The goal is to become a relational adult whose love increases and overflows toward others. First Thessalonians 3:12 says, "May the Lord make your love increase and overflow for each other, and for everyone else just as ours does for you."

We begin the journey by receiving enough love to become rooted in love and form our first relational lens—*the bonding lens*. Through the bonding lens, we can perceive ourselves as beloved even when those who love us are not physically present. Our ability to bond signals our ability to store enough love to stay related to others over the fear of abandonment.

Bonding is the main supply route for giving and receiving love, especially during disagreements and conflicts. The Bible calls this becoming perfected or rooted in love: "There is no fear in love. But perfect love drives out fear, because fear has to do with punishment. The one who fears is not made perfect in love" (1 John 4:18). Paul prayed that the church of Ephesus would be rooted in love: "so that Christ may dwell in your heart through faith, and I pray that you are being rooted and established in love" (Ephesians 3:17).

Once bonded in love, we embark on discovering boundaries and forming our identity. In establishing our identity, we experience separateness from others and relate to them through *the distinctness lens*. We claim our position in God as joint heirs who are free and privileged: "I am a joint heir with Christ" (Romans 8:17). As a result, we grow in freedom and responsibility. A bonus is we also learn to take the initiative and build trust.

Afterward, we accept our flaws and confess them truthfully to others: "Therefore each of you must put off falsehood and speak truthfully to your neighbor, for we are all members of one body" (Ephesians 4:25). James 5:15 (AMP) says, "Confess to one another, therefore your faults and pray for one another that you may be healed and restored."

As a result of receiving grace from others, we no longer hide or change our behavior in secret or public; we become integrated. Luke 12:2 says, "Nothing is covered up that it will not be revealed or hidden that it will not be known." In becoming integrated, we relate through *the integration lens* and accept others as unique despite their shortcomings.

Finally, we grow in power and experience and become level or equal with others. We learn both submission and delegation of authority. We are ready to serve, lead, and practice the authority conferred to us by Jesus. He said in Luke 22:29, "And as My Father has appointed a kingdom and conferred it on Me, so do I confer on you." Through *the levelness lens*, we perceive others as equal to us in worth.

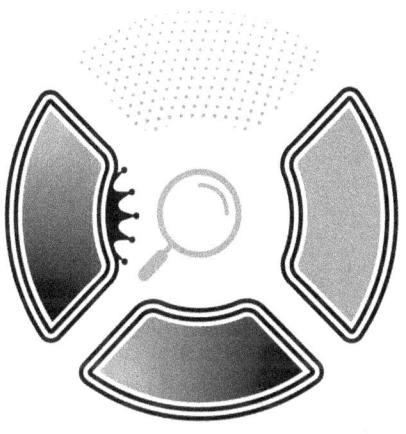

Figure 1 depicts the four relational lenses

Figure 1 depicts the relationship lenses starting with the bonding lens at 12 o'clock, the distinctness lens at 3 o'clock, the integration lens at 6 o'clock, and levelness lens at 9 o'clock.

The Relational Stages

Relational growth requires love, grace, and truthful feedback. It is not automatic. If we suffer harm, we experience an arrest in our development. We continue to use deformed lenses that no longer meet our evolving needs. Relational delay becomes more debilitating because relational needs to increase.

If we do not receive enough love deposits to become bonded, as a result, we relate through an abandonment lens. Childhood emotional injuries delay forming boundaries and establishing distinct identities. We adopt a deformed lens such as devaluation or compliance.

If we do not resolve the inner conflict between our virtues and our flaws, we relate through the splitting lens, through which we experience others as exclusively good or bad. Finally, we do not level with others. We link to them through disparity lenses from above or under. We do not perceive them as equally worthy and free.

Relational Stage	Sound Lens	Deformed Lens
Rooted in love	bonding	abandonment
Identity formation	distinctness	devaluation/compliance
Resolving the inner conflict	integration	splitting
Level position	levelness	disparity

Table 1: Relational Stages and the Corresponding Lenses

We all need to be loved, heard, and understood. We can see those needs met solely within the realm of relationships. Through sound lenses, we relate to others in ways that honor them and respect their freedom and equality while still meeting our needs.

In relating through the deformed lenses, however, we inevitably dishonor others or violate their freedom, damaging our relationship with them. The results are that we do not receive love, listening, or understanding from them. We live strained and unfulfilled lives despite our good intentions and attempts to do the right thing. As the rift in our relationships widens, we become frantic with the pain of past losses and dread of future ones. Our gradual loss of relationships can catapult us into complete isolation. It is not uncommon for relational death to usher in physical death.

We cannot satisfy our relational needs by accumulating accomplishments, accolades, or followers on social media. We see startling news at times about famed influencers or ordinary people ending their lives, which is a reflection of the sheer pain, despair, and isolation they experienced before tragedy struck.

In Matthew 6:22, Jesus described the eye as the body's lamp. He stated, "The eye is the lamp of the body. So if your eye is sound, your entire body will be full of light." Jesus said the way we see others is consequential. It dictates whether we will enjoy the light of love or stumble in the darkness of offense.

Jesus brought the good news that there is hope, and we can overcome our problems in relating. "His divine power has given us everything we need for life and godliness through our knowledge of him who called us by his glory and goodness" (2 Peter 1:3).

Are you curious to know at which stage you or your loved ones fit in? Let's go deeper into each stage. We will begin with the first stage, which is becoming rooted in love.

7

Rooted in Love

Loved Then Lovable

"He won't feed or stop crying," the nurse said. She was referring to a newborn infant we had in our care. The young mother had domestic problems and could not be there for her baby.

The little one was kicking, screaming, and sweating. My colleague had ordered medication to help, but I did not think this was effective. I requested one of our seasoned volunteers to come to our aid. The experienced volunteer quickly picked up the infant and spoke to him softly as she rocked him gently.

With her gentle provision and caring, she soothed the infant. What a remarkable turnaround! The infant chugged a couple of ounces of milk and went to sleep peacefully. Observing the incident affirmed my awareness of how love deposits are given through connecting and providing.

Like this newborn, our relational growth launches when we are embraced by parents (or caregivers) who connect and provide for us. We feel terror as soon as we are born. We spent long months napping in a quiet, dark place. We suddenly find ourselves in the heart of noise and light. We see strange faces and hear unintelligible sounds. We desperately search for someone to be with. We hear a familiar voice and feel someone hugging us. She is our mom. We attach to her with all our strength. We do not imagine what it's like to be away from her. We think we are one with her. We experience isolation when she is missing. We cry and kick to communicate what we want. We want to be cuddled and reassured. We do not recognize our mom's provision for our needs. For example, when she breastfeeds us, we think we are doing the bulk of the work of feeding. Every time we cry for a need and receive a provision from our mom, we store a small installment of love. It is a love deposit.

We need to store enough love deposits to withstand the occasions when our mom leaves. When we perceive ourselves as beloved in the absence of our mom, we develop what is called emotional permanency. We can still relate or bond with our mom even when we do not see her. *See Figure 2.*

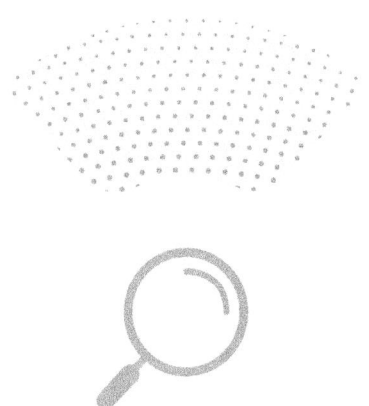

Figure 2 depicts the bonding lens

The Bonding Lens

We need to store enough love to perceive our state of being loved when we are alone. Afterward, we form the bonding lens through which we can remain connected with others we do not see so we no longer feel terror when our loved ones are not with us. We don't panic and look for another to connect with. Being able to store love is a requisite before we can pursue adventures (on foot!) and explore the world (the living room!).

We exercise our newly formed lens by staying engaged in

trustworthy friendships. They hold us up when we stumble. According to Ecclesiastes 4:10, "If either of them falls, one can help the other up, but pity anyone who falls and has no one to help them up." Romans 12:10 says, "Be devoted to one another in love. Honor one another above yourselves." Those who don't treasure friendships are unlikely to succeed in other relationships like romance or parenting.

The Apostle Paul understood becoming rooted in God's love to be an experience more than a piece of head knowledge. He said in Ephesians 3:19, "To know this love, that surpasses knowledge that you may be filled to the measure of all the fullness of God."

We want to challenge the myth of conditional love that may have been passed to us from our family. It is the myth that bases our feeling beloved on what we achieve. Nothing is further from the truth. God loves us due to His loving character: "And so we know, and rely on the love God has for us. God is love; whoever lives in love lives in God and God in them" (1 John 4:16).

No services or charitable deeds can qualify us for His love. Instead, His love for us is the touchstone from which we sprint to ownership, freedom, and service. To the extent we receive unmerited love deposits from God and others, we can bestow it on others.

We need to make conscientious efforts to bond with our children. As parents, we want to begin relating to the fetus as soon as we learn about conception. We can obtain a printout of their image during the obstetrics ultrasound scan and display the picture on a fridge or bathroom mirror, so we can often gaze at it. We can read them a book, even joke with them when they kick strongly inside us. At birth, we reach out to touch and hug them. We look into their eyes and recite words of value, welcome, and reassurance. These fragile creatures rely wholeheartedly on us to get their love deposits.

Physical presence is a top priority for bonding. We need to take an extended vacation and shelve all but the most necessary chores. We should aim to spend ample time connecting and providing for our baby. We must deal with mood changes and also the shifting dynamics with the extended family. Bonding requires consistently giving love deposits. As a result we will marvel at the magical transformation of babies into sons and daughters. We will feel profound joy and contentment as we recognize God's gift of life and love.

Medical professionals need to prioritize infant bonding and recognize the hindering impact of our exams and assessments. We need to facilitate alternate ways of the parents bonding with them should the infant need complex medical care.

The Abandonment Lens

When we receive enough love deposits, we bond with our parents. Through *the bonding lens*, we can relate to them when they leave. It helps us store their love, so when we depart from their presence we are able to explore. If we endure the loss or absence of our caregiver, we do not receive love. We suffer abandonment and do not learn to bond with others.

Through *the abandonment lens*, we do not perceive that we are beloved. We approach others in fear that they might abandon us too. When our partners leave our presence, we feel unloved and lonely. We can't stay connected with them during disagreements. We feel flooded with fear of being alone; we waste no time clinging to new partners. Those who were abandoned, in turn, inflict abandonment on their partners in the future. They often open themselves to irresponsible and relationally risky individuals.

The abandonment lens cuts into our relationships with family and close ones, depriving us of love and gratitude. As a result, we don't claim our self-value and indict ourselves for every error. Once we store enough guilty verdicts, we start issuing them to others too.

Without bonding with others, we regress to connecting with material things. We hope they will meet our needs to be loved; however, no amount of possessions can fill the void, so we continue hoarding more of everything.

In abandonment, our emotional state resembles a roller-coaster. Fear dominates us, and often we feel anger for blocking it. The pain of repeated breakups adds to the misery.

Our short, shallow relationships fail, and we eventually end up in isolation, losing honest feedback from others. We struggle with illusions and a long list of mental disorders as well as addiction and violence.

On the other hand, Romans 8:1 points the way when it says, "Therefore, there is no condemnation for those in Christ." These are the ones who are simply bonded with agape love.

The apostle Paul said that we "can do all things through Christ Jesus" (Philippians 4:13). How can we learn to bond while we are abandoned? Being a member of the medical community, I have treated many malnourished kids. We initially feed them in small amounts, gradually increasing the amounts and treat them for existing infections. When we are abandoned, we are malnourished emotionally. We need the emotional nutrition of love deposits over time, so we shed the abandonment lens and put on *the bonding lens*. We also need healing from the harm of previous failed relationships.

The process is exciting but lengthy—it can take months or even years! Impatient as we are, this sounds disheartening, but we need to persevere and remember that the stakes are very high. Bonding is the conduit for living a life of connectedness, contentment, and service.

We seek love deposits from trustworthy others who relate through bonding and distinctness lenses. Their looks, profession, or prestige do not matter. What matters is that they have stored enough love deposits and can deposit them into us through words and deeds of honor. Through *the distinctness lens*, they respect our freedom and avoid manipulation, control, or judgment. We resist fusing with them and reject the illusion that they are responsible for us. We won't withdraw from them during disagreements.

Someone may object that we have not yet learned how to distinguish trust. It is a valid question. We can seek help from therapists and church friends for their advice and truthful feedback. We need patience and humility as we let the Holy Spirit guide us to the trustworthy, loving saints with whom we can bond. First Corinthians 1:9 says, "God is faithful, by Him you were called into companionship and participation with His Son, Jesus Christ our Lord."

Many who suffered abandonment don't know where to start. They repeat the same pattern of opening themselves to manipulating or controlling others. We must guard ourselves by avoiding relationships with risky others. They are bound to expose us to the harms of betrayal and rejection, which increases our delay.

We need to understand the risk of romantic relationships with their deeper connections and higher chances of emotional hurt and harm. We better avoid romance until we grow to relate through the distinctness lens and learn how to build trust.

The Holy Spirit does not invade us with His love. He eagerly meets us as soon as we seek Him. We focus on being still, so we receive His agape love deposits and experience His affirmation of us. Seeking the Holy Spirit in solitude is vital, but it is not a replacement for seeking love deposits from His bondservants.

Perhaps one of the most stunning revelations about God is that He does not abandon us when we sin against Him. Jeremiah

51:5 reads, "Neither Israel nor Judah has been abandoned by his God the Lord of the host, though their land is full of sin and guilt before the holy one of Israel."

God is holy, and despite His holiness, He grieves over our sins against Him without abandoning us. God stays bonded with us to give us grace, truth, and forgiveness. We can accomplish God's callings only when we are rooted in Him. He is the vine, and we are the branches: "I am the vine; you are the branches. If you remain in me and I in you, you will bear much fruit; apart from me you can do nothing" (John 15:5).

In bonding with others and God, we claim our position of being beloved, but that is just the beginning. What comes next is more exciting. We shall build distinct identities and learn freedom and responsibility. Let's see how it is done in the next chapter.

8

Distinct not Obscure

Forming an Identity

"Oh no!" John, my toddler, wailed. Looking closely, I noticed his Spider-Man action figure had lost a leg. I am thinking, *I just bought this thing yesterday. Was it worth the money or the time spent standing in line to check out with it at the crowded store?*

Hoping to save the day (and Spider-Man), I picked up the severed leg and tried to reattach it. Unfortunately, as I applied pressure, the leg broke in half. John, with tears welling in his eyes, asked, "What happened, Dad? What happened?"

I said,"Spider-Man's leg broke. Sorry, it's my fault."

"The fault is not yours," he said. "It's mine."

Trying hard not to laugh, I said, "Let's go back to the store and get an exchange."

I thought, *My toddler wants to possess everything, including my mistake.* Toddlers may not know what something is, but they want to own it. They do not know boundaries.

In the previous chapter, we learned that we become emotionally stable through receiving love deposits. Once we store enough deposits, we withstand the absence of our loving caretaker and perceive ourselves as beloved.

Armed with the perception of being loved, we explore the world. We survey our surroundings, touch things, and put whatever we touch in our mouth. What a sensational adventure. We experiment, even for seconds, getting away from our mom. It seems that she and we are not one person.

We feel capable of exploring everywhere, doing anything, and getting all we want. Our power has no limits. The whole world is our backyard. We know no self-control and accept no delays in gratifying ourselves.

We feel sad and angry when we do not get what we want. Our mother helps solve this predicament; she affirms her love and explains that we cannot always get all we want. Feeling the limits, we return to our fusion with our mom again. Her loving embrace helps us accept the difficult reality that the world is not ours.

We need to distinguish ourselves from Mom. It looks as if wielding the word no will allow us to do that. We start replying with *no* to whatever we are asked. We respond especially with no when requested to share our toys.

When we say no, we observe our parents' responses. If they affirm their love for us, we feel safe and better define ourselves and know our possessions. We sometimes hear our parents say no to each other. We monitor how they respond to each other's no. We learn that respecting others' no is as important as respecting them.

We delight when our parents affirm their respect for our possessions. It is a tangible step for us to learn about responsibility. We then can grow from being responsible for material things to being accountable for immaterial things like time, emotions, and thoughts.

Figure 3 depicts the distinctness lens

The Distinctness Lens

Once we store enough love deposits, we venture away to differentiate ourselves from our parents. We discover ourselves by distinguishing what is us and what is everything else. We use our no to determine what is not us. When our parents respond to our no with affirmation and love, we recognize our boundaries and form our distinctness lens.

In relating through distinctness, we approach others as separate from us. We comprehend the need to convey our thoughts and emotions to them so they will understand and respect us. We increasingly use our no to disagree with others and protect ourselves from false responsibilities. We learn the responsible use of no before we learn the free use of *yes* to agree. Jesus praised the first son, who initially refused to help his father in the vineyard, but later took responsibility for his refusal and changed his mind and went to help: "What do you think? There was a man who had two sons. He went to the first and said. 'Son, go and work today in the vineyard.' 'I will not,' he answered, but later he changed his mind and went" (Matthew 21:28-29). The other son was irresponsible because he did not follow through when he said yes (Matthew 21:30).

When we experience our distinctness, we own our illusions and the resulting harmful behaviors. The Holy Spirit is the Spirit of Truth, and He imparts His word so we can renew our minds and have the mind of Christ (Philippians 2:5; 1 Corinthians 2:16).

God relays the truth through His trustworthy saints who are not afraid of displeasing us. We need humility and forbearance to receive candid feedback and free ourselves from illusions. Jesus told the disciples in John 8:32, "Then you will know the truth, and the truth will set you free."

We want to significantly challenge the victimhood illusion, which denies the use of will and blames others. The victimhood illusion is a self-fulfilling prophecy. It works as follows:

Perceiving ourselves as victims, we approach situations flooded with fear and let others decide on our behalf. Later, we get harmed by the result of their decisions and prove our point about being victimized.

We shouldn't blame others when we experience harm in our relationship with them. We need to understand our responsibility for opening ourselves to them and agreeing to their requests. An offense is a relational transaction, and its responsibility is divided between both parties. We bear our share, and others own theirs. The Apostle Paul experienced the desertion of his friends: "At my first defense, no one came to my support, but everyone deserted me. May it not be held against them" (2 Timothy 4:16).

We shouldn't blame our parents for our illusions. As equal adults, we must prevail over our illusions, so we won't pass them on to our offspring. We should not blame our childhood injustices for our emotional outbursts of today. We should not deny our past injuries nor try to rewrite them. We need to express our painful memories to wholehearted listeners, who offer us empathy, truth, and encouragement. Our current perceptions of the former injuries contribute more to our pain than the injuries themselves.

We shouldn't blame certain words or phrases for our explosive behavior. We should re-examine our prior experience with the trigger phrase and understand our emotional outburst when the phrase was directed toward us. We can now observe how others respond differently to the phrase and attach the new response to it. We eventually want to disarm all provocative phrases, words, or names so they can no longer affect us.

Through the distinctness lens, we learn to take risks and build trust with others. Trust is a dynamic cycle of giving recipients credibility and experiencing their faithfulness. We always need to deepen our trust with someone before disclosing the vulnerable parts of ourselves.

When we relate through the distinctness lens, we realize who we are and invite others to be themselves also. We then become free to have friendships, romance, and more importantly, serve. Finally, the distinctness lens is vital to us as parents so that we can deliberately transfer responsibility to our children. We should bestow unconditional love on them so they can withstand the assigned responsibility. We want our children to experience responsibility and grow to be distinct and equal adults.

The Compliance and Devaluation Lenses

Love flows between distinct partners, with each owning their responsibilities. Others who relate through the distinctness lens respect our refusals and value our courage to be truthful. They comprehend that when we use our no, we aim to safeguard our hearts.

When we are toddlers exploring our boundaries, if our parents withdraw their love in response to our no, we feel terrorized. Fearing we might lose, we avoid saying no and comply to secure their love. This is the birth of the *compliance lens*.

Scripture emphasizes speaking the truth to each other, so we and others mature in Christ. "Speaking the truth in love, we will grow to become in every respect the mature body of Him who is the head, that is, Christ" (Ephesians 4:15). In relating through the compliance lens, we conceal the truth about our disagreements and do not express our differences. We fear that saying no to others will displease others and cost us the loss of their love.

Saying no is necessary to guard our hearts: "Above all, guard your heart for everything you do flows from it" (Proverbs 4:23). Through the compliance lens, we begrudgingly agree with the results of others' irresponsible decisions. As a result the additional emotional toll drowns us in depression and resentment. On a deeper level, our compliance stems from failing to form a solid identity. With our identity seat vacant, we embrace false identities. We crown others as role models and accept their beliefs and attitudes. Paul warned the Corinthians about this: "Do not be misled: bad company corrupts good character" (1 Corinthians 15:33).

Compliance and Vague Identity

Without an identity, we don't uncover our treasures and wind up envying others for their talents. We waste energy and time watching others and wishing to live their lives. We need to sharpen our identity, and in the process, unearth our own talents. Proverb 27:17 says, "As iron sharpens iron, so one person sharpens another." We lean on the Holy Spirit and the trustworthy saints for truth and wisdom that help the sharpening.

Once we discover our talents, we should nurture them with time, money, and resources. Growing our talents is the journey of our thankfulness to God for them and not a competition with others.

Another adverse effect of lacking a distinct identity is that we don't recognize the jurisdiction of power and responsibility. As a result, we relate to others through the devaluation lens.

Through *the devaluation lens*, we violate others' freedom and coerce them into taking on our responsibilities. We act irresponsibly and expect others to take the fall. When they decline (rightfully so!), we resort to threats and maybe violence. If they comply, we fuse with them, dreaming they will be our ticket to maturity. The illusion invariably fails because responsibility and growth cannot be outsourced.

The devaluation lens may take more subtle patterns, like luring others to do our bidding, or sulking to force them to read our minds. The Scripture asks us to speak the truth in love to one another (Ephesians 4:15).

Some assume that sharing truthfulness with others will harm them. Our motive behind speaking the truth is to invite them to responsibility, not harm them. We want to be kind and honor others before disclosing the truth to them, but we are not responsible for their responses.

The Holy Spirit relates to us in freedom and distinctness. He doesn't do what we are responsible for doing, nor does He rescue us from the consequences of our choices. He loves and admonishes us to grow, so He delegated us as Christ's ambassadors: "I am an ambassador of Christ" (2 Corinthians 5:20). Patience is one of the fruits of the Spirit; we shouldn't hold off fulfilling our responsibility with the false expectation that He will graciously intervene and do our part.

As a young Christian, I was taught to sacrifice my life for others. The teaching was based on Luke 14:27: "Whoever does not carry the cross, and follow me, cannot be my disciple." Nonetheless, I now have my own take on that teaching. I believe Jesus implores us to carry the cross and follow His lead in submission to the Father.

I don't consider carrying the cross equivalent to sacrificing my life on behalf of others. Jesus sacrificed Himself, knowing that His assignment was to be the holy propitiation for our sins. He fulfilled His part in the Father's divine plan of redemption.

Similarly, we want to receive our assignment from the Holy Spirit before jumping to sacrifice ourselves on behalf of others. I believe we are more helpful to God when we are alive, at least to a point!

Forming an identity is exciting. But what sort of identity do we have? Is it all virtuous, or does it have flaws? The answer lies in our next growth stage. Stay tuned.

9

Unique Despite Flaws

Splitting into All Good or Bad

I enjoy receiving appreciation cards from satisfied parents. It is rewarding to see the fragile little ones thriving. I was on my break reading a card when I heard Kate say, "It makes me sick to see acts like this." A nurse aide, Kate was watching the news on the TV in the room. The grainy clip showed some teens snatching a mobile phone from an elderly Asian man in an urban square. As we both stared at the screen, Kate's phone blasted musical tunes, and she quickly answered.

My hearing is average (in my good ear!). But the male caller's voice was loud. He was complaining that neighbors had parked their cars in his designated spot. Kate answered him. "Honey, they are probably a newly moved immigrant couple. They don't have a clue about rules!"

My coworker is appalled by someone's discriminatory behavior, yet she displays prejudice in her attitude. We can argue that her strong aversion to a flaw in others is that she has not overcome the same flaw in herself. She perceives her virtue but not her flaws. She is splitting between them. She had not resolved her inner conflict.

In this chapter, we will address recognizing our flaws and reconciling them. In doing so, we settle our inner conflict.

The Integration Lens

As we shared in earlier chapters, we begin our emotional development by storing enough love to bond with others. In relating to our caregivers through the bonding lens, we feel loved despite their physical absence. We then venture out, learn our boundaries, and relate through the distinctness lens. We evolve in freedom and responsibility and shed the distorted lenses of devaluation and compliance.

Having perceived our distinctness, we sense a dilemma. People do not seem to be what they pretend to be. They are different on the inside from what they display on the outside. We are alarmed to see righteous people committing wicked deeds. This dilemma seems like a puzzle we cannot solve. What is the truth about others? Are others bad but pretending to be good? Perhaps even more perplexing, are we good or bad on the inside?

We remember the time on our mother's breasts. We perceived her to be good when she nursed us but thought she was wicked when she left the room, while we were crying. It seems we experienced her good at times and evil at others. We just exclusively experienced each side alone. We split between the good and bad sides.

We readily brag about our goodness. However, can we have wickedness too, but we do not detect it? Is it possible that we meticulously split between our inner good and evil? We may be terrified that if the bad were to mix with the good, all would be ruined.

We need truthful feedback from our trustworthy friends to recognize our flaws. Ephesians 4:15 says, "Instead, speaking the truth in love, we will grow to become in every respect the mature body of him who is the head that is Christ." The Holy Spirit is the Spirit of Truth. He affirms us with His love before He conveys our flaws.

In recognizing our flaws, we grieve the loss of our old perceptions. The sadness we embrace signals a new room inside ourselves that we can use to accept more loving and responsible perceptions. We shouldn't attempt to evade sadness at any price, for that will make us falsely cheerful and aggravate our flaws. It's only after we learn how to grieve our weaknesses wholeheartedly that we can celebrate our strengths joyfully.

Some of our flaws are false and stem from the distorted perception of our legitimate needs. For example, we may assume that our need for intimacy is shameful. But it is a need that is legitimate and worthy of provision. Or we may indict ourselves for feeling angry instead of accepting our angry responses and recognizing our demands. We may speculate that pleasing any of our desires is selfish, which also is not necessarily true. Fulfilling some desires, if done responsibly and patiently, can be joyful. "Longing fulfilled is sweet to the soul, but fools detest, turning from evil" (Proverb 13:19).

We have to be mindful that we have genuine flaws. We do commit injustice, act selfishly, or devalue others at times. We can resolve our inner conflict by disclosing our flaws truthfully. James 5:16 says, "Confess to one another therefore your fault and pray for one another's that you may be healed and restored."

The recipients of our disclosure should be those who have settled their inner conflict. They have received grace for their flaws, and therefore, can administer grace to us: "Who comforts us in all our troubles, so that we can comfort those in any trouble with the comfort we ourselves receive from God" (2 Corinthians 1:4). We don't condemn ourselves nor accept others' condemnation.

The gracious saints see us as genuinely good despite our flaws. It is the grace that we receive that makes us able to say no to flaws. Titus 2:12 says, "It teaches us to say no to ungodliness and worldly passions, and to live self-controlled, upright, and godly lives in this present age."

I suggest using the word *I* in disclosing flaws. It conveys power and willingness to accept responsibility for flawed choices. There is no room to make excuses, blame others, or play the victim.

Acceptance does not negate disagreement. When gracious, integrated others accept us, they still don't approve of our flaws. They love the whole of us more than being repulsed by our weaknesses. We can harness their grace and love to face our flaws.

As we allow grace to displace shame, our flawed parts merge gradually with the good ones. We become uniquely integrated, like a mosaic piece. Once we perceive ourselves as genuine treasures, we can see others through the integration lens. See Figure 4.

Figure 4 depicts the integration lens

In becoming authentic, we recognize how our flaws harm our ability to walk in love. They swarm the love motive and usurp time and energy.

Our flawed desires are replaceable. As we challenge the illusions that feed them, we cease to be infatuated with their secretive allure. We can attain new desires that are aligned with the love motive.

A word of caution—a behavior, even a wicked one, caters to desires or needs. When we quit, we create a dangerous vacuum that can be used for addiction or violence. We need to prevent the vacuum by letting new genuine behavior displace the old flawed ones.

Jesus cautioned against the danger of the vacuum being used by the evil spirit: "Then it says, 'I will return to my house from where I came. It finds the place unoccupied, swept, and put in order. Then it goes and brings with it seven other spirits more wicked than itself'" (Matthew 12:44).

Going forward, we celebrate the courage of those who relate through the integration lens. They are unique. They do not hide their scars but see them as trophies of overcoming. Despite relational setbacks, they continue to deepen trust and love others. They don't let their flaws prevent them from serving and loving. They learn to dialogue with their good and part parts, revere the good, and shun the bad. "Do not be wise in your eyes; fear the Lord and shun evil" (Proverb 3:7).

When we relate through the integration lens, we treasure others as a whole without focusing on their stumbling. We relate to the whole, not the part. We notice how Jesus responded to John the Baptist, who sent his disciples to inquire whether Jesus was the Messiah. Jesus did not indict John's doubtful query, but He graciously praised John in front of the crowd: "But what did you go out to see? A prophet? Yes, I tell you, and more than a prophet" (Luke 7:26). Jesus saw him as a whole, fulfilling his assignment as the messenger.

Lastly, we shouldn't confuse integration with perfection. Love patiently guides us to integration, but fear demands perfection. We need to give up the demands for perfection and celebrate others who are integrated.

The Splitting Lens

Having perceived our distinctness, we form an identity. But soon after, we face the dilemma of dealing with the bad parts of our identity. We resort to separating the experience of good and evil inside us.

When we have not dealt with a particular flaw inside us, we strongly detest it in others. It is a telltale sign of the split inside us. In splitting, we disavow the terrible parts of ourselves and conceal them. The problem is that it does not abolish their influence. They breed secret addictions and obsessions. We cater to those dark hidden habits while we nurture a virtuous visible side.

Over time, we have split into two people: one lives in public and another in secrecy. We fail to become authentic and resort to relating through the splitting lens.

Splitting into Good or Bad

Through the splitting lens, we divide others and situations as all evil or all good. This causes our behavior to swing radically toward or away from them.

Peter behaved differently toward the Gentiles when people of the circumcision arrived. Paul rebuked him in Galatians 2:12: "For before certain men came from James. He used to eat with the Gentiles, but when they arrived, he began to draw back and separate himself from the Gentiles." Part of Peter loved the Gentiles as saints, but his splitting parts still perceived eating with them as sinful.

We may split between intention and attitude. We focus on the legitimacy of our intentions but neglect empathy and kindness in our conduct toward others. Jesus rebuked the Pharisees who prided themselves in following the laws but neglected mercy:

Woe to you, teachers of the law and Pharisees, you hypocrites! You give a tenth of your spices—mint, dill and cumin. But you have neglected the more important matters of the law—justice, mercy, and faithfulness. You should have prac-

ticed the latter, without neglecting the former (Matthew 23:23).

In splitting, we assume that the part we experience about others represents the whole of them. Therefore, we misjudge their trustworthiness. As soon as we experience their virtues, we lavish our trust on them. Later, as soon as they err, we experience them as unreliable and withdraw our trust. This change resembles making a relational U-turn. It ignites conflicts and implodes the relationship.

Jesus did not withdraw His trust from Peter when the latter betrayed Him. Shortly after the resurrection, He asked Peter to feed His lambs (John: 21:15). We can pause, deepening trust and inviting growth, but we won't hastily conclude that they are entirely untrustworthy.

In mistaking the part for the whole, we confuse others' emotions for their character. For example, we experience someone's pleasantness in a situation, and we conclude that they have a good character. But Proverb 5:3 warns that lips can drip honey, but the person can be bitter and cutting.

Splitting skews our perception of God's character. We perceive God as loving when He provides for us but perceive Him to be unloving when He disciplines us. The truth is God doesn't stop loving us when He disciplines us as His children: "Know then in your hearts that as a man disciplines and instructs his son, so the Lord your God disciplines and instructs you" (Deuteronomy 8:5).

The deceiver uses splitting to hinder us from receiving healing. But the Holy Spirit heals us in degrees, and as a result, we change from glory to glory (2 Corinthians 3:18). The Holy Spirit never stops healing.

Our gracious God loves us as a whole and doesn't drown in our flaws. "I have rolled away the reproach of Egypt from you.

So the place has been called Gilgal (rolling) to this day" (Joshua 5:9).

Claim your Gilgal, receive grace, and administer grace. Christ's body is an amazing tapestry of unique saints. That is why we need to relate to others as equals and the next chapter will guide us through it.

10

Level Leaders

Stand Up to Leaders

Not again! I said to myself, as I read an email from the billing department about a duplicate claim. My frustration grew because the issue had happened many times. Our computer was aging, not gracefully if you ask me! It randomly pre-checks some orders, and when a provider checks an order, a duplicate claim is submitted.

My boss, the chief medical officer, emailed me, questioning why I billed twice. It felt as if he laid the responsibility for the error on my doorstep. I rejected the urge to email him back immediately. I took a few deep breaths and carried on with my work at the next c-section.

Wolfing down my salad during my lunch break, I felt ready to answer his email. I opened by thanking him for the feedback, then I said, "I would have liked your feedback to include other possibilities for the error occurring. Those include a computer glitch or accounting error, besides the possibility on my end." The chief, to his credit, accepted my confrontation and promised to investigate the billing process.

It was a work situation involving medical billing. I perceived myself to be level with the chief, despite his occupying the position of authority. I stood up to him, both respecting him as a person and questioning how he used his position of authority.

This chapter addresses others as equals regardless of their

authority or power. This is the final stage of relational maturity. It represents relational adulthood.

Authority and Delegating Responsibility

We grow in our ability to relate from bonding to relating through the distinctness lens. We then resolve our inner conflict and relate through the *integration lens*. We continue to grow in experience, skill, and resources. We become prepared to manage authority.

We understand authority to be the power to lead others in civil, vocational, and professional venues. It protects others' freedoms and transfers responsibility to them so they multiply, grow, and dominate the earth. Our dealing with power goes back to early childhood. We experienced our mom's power when she protected us. We, therefore, associate power with protection.

Later in childhood, we observed our father as an authority figure. We felt annoyed, to be honest, when he deterred us from doing what we wanted to do. However, our father affirmed our values before guiding us. We watched him abide by the principles he guided us with.

During our teen years, our parents gave us more freedom to choose. They did not rescind their love when we were hurtful or irresponsible. Instead, they exhorted us to assume responsibility for our acts and continued loving us. Their unwavering love helped us endure the consequences of our actions without feeling punished. They used their authority to help us to become more responsible and independent.

We comprehend how our parents used their authority to raise us. In becoming equal to them, we occupy the same position. We comprehend the positional nature of authority.

We are to honor leaders and intercede on their behalf for wisdom, mercy, and righteousness. First Timothy 2:1-2 (AMP) says,

"First of all, then, I urge that petitions, prayers, intercessions and thanksgivings be offered on behalf of all people, for kings and all who in authority that we may live a peaceful and quiet life in all godliness and dignity."

Scripture gives us a balanced guide. On one hand, we need to submit to authority. Romans 13:1 says, "Let everyone be subject to the governing authorities, for there is no authority, except that which God has established the authorities that exist have been established by God." On the other hand, submitting is done freely and responsibly. We can disagree with authority rules if they are not consistent with God's commands. In Mark 7:9 (NKJV), Jesus chastised the Pharisees for using their position to discard God's commands: "All too well you reject the Commandments of God, that you may keep your tradition."

In submitting to authority, we submit to the position, not the person. We are level with authority figures as people but are different from them in position.

God commanded us to grow and multiply: "Be fruitful and increase in number; fill the earth and subdue it" (Genesis 1:28). He asked to increase the fellowship of love: "May the Lord make your love increase and overflow for each other, and for everyone else just as ours for you" (1 Thessalonians 3:12).

When occupying the authority position, we want to transfer responsibility to trustworthy subordinates so they can fulfill God-designed tasks for humans. Jesus delegated authority to disciples: "Behold! I have given you authority and power to trample upon serpents and scorpions, and [physical and mental strength and ability] over all the power that the enemy [possesses]; and nothing shall in any way harm you" (Luke 10:19).

We desire the recipient of the delegated authority to be one of those who formed a solid identity. We comprehend the risks of delegating them with responsibility.

It is vital that we relate through the distinctness lens in the delegation process. We are responsible for guiding subordinates, correcting them, and deploying consequences if they commit egregious negligence. Delegating responsibility frees us as leaders to inspire and create new aims. Failing to delegate responsibility leads us to trespass on subordinates' boundaries in an attempt to do their work or what we call micromanaging. They own the delegated responsibility and will need to increase in love, power, and experience.

As leaders, we want to recognize that subordinates' relational maturity dictates the way they experience discipline. When they are bonded in love, they experience discipline as a predictable result of their choices. As a result, they expand in responsibility, humility, and empathy toward others. In contrast, if they have not claimed their beloved state, they have already inaugurated an inner judge and are likely to perceive consequences as punishments.

We are not responsible for the subordinates' experience of discipline. But we need to affirm their irreducible value and refrain from condemning their choice. If they experience the discipline as a cruel penalty, we clarify our intent to grow them in responsibility.

Proverbs 19:18 says, "Discipline and teach your son while there is hope, and do not [indulge your anger or resentment by imposing inappropriate punishment nor] desire his destruction." And Proverbs 28:23 says, "He who rebukes a man shall afterward find more favor than he who flatters with the tongue."

The Levelness Lens

We evolve in our ability to make independent decisions. We evaluate others' opinions in light of our beliefs, wisdom, and experiences. We learn to employ our insight and logic together to form our best decisions.

We eventually adopt an equal position with others. We relate to them through the levelness lens and experience parity with them. We are unique in our virtues and reconciled flaws. Others are too. We can stand with them in their adversity and defy them in their cruelty.

Figure 5 depicts the levelness lens

Through the levelness lens (see Figure 5), we honor others as equally worthy, regardless of their title or achievement. Leveling signals our capacity to perceive the positional nature of authority and parenting.

Individuals occupy the authority position to protect and guide others. We comprehend that practicing authority is a noble form of serving others. When we relate to authority through the levelness lens, we understand that in honoring authority figures, the honor is given to their position. Similarly, when we solicit clarifications from them, we recognize the limits of the authority of their position.

We need to win our freedom before we deliberately relinquish some of it to submit to the authority position. Submission is done responsibly out of reverence to Christ: "Submit to one another out of reverence for Christ."

God does not violate His loving and just nature; therefore, we can disobey authority decrees that are irresponsible or unjust. Our intention in submitting is to receive more responsibility, so we can love and serve others better.

Jesus warned soldiers in Luke 3:14: "And the soldiers likewise demanded of him, saying, and what shall we do, and he said unto them do violence to no man neither accuse any falsely, and be content with your wages." We shouldn't leverage fear or threats to force obedience. In blindly obeying out of fear, we step outside of the realm of our responsibility to love others.

We shouldn't blindly obey rules, for they should have been authored to serve love. On the other hand, love shouldn't be the causality for obedience. If our parents use guilt to secure our obedience, we learn to obey so we experience being righteous. Paul clarifies that our righteousness is a gracious gift from Jesus: "That as sin rained in death so also grace, reign through righteousness to bring eternal life through Jesus Christ our lord" (Romans 5:21). We want to perceive our beloved, righteous state with God, so we do not use obeying rules as a means to holiness. There are no guilty verdicts against us because of the blood of Jesus. Hallelujah!

As leaders, we don't seek only those who agree with us all the time. We need different perspectives from subordinates who relate through the levelness lens. They aren't afraid of disagreeing with us but see it as an opportunity to enrich our vision. They recognize that occupying the position of authority is not a goal but a means to serve.

In regard to intimacy, our parents may have taught us that intimacy is shameful. In leveling with them, we need to challenge this teaching and accept the need for intimacy as righteous.

Relating through the levelness lens is essential in romantic love. We need to give our romantic partner equal time in hearing and resolving conflict. Romantic love flourishes only between level partners. Levelness induces us to respect others' spiritual beliefs or gender orientation. We won't morally classify their choice, nor use logic to reason it.

Jesus led from the level position: "He went down with them

and stood on a level spot" (Luke 6:17). He did not need a huge podium to command power. After all, He knew His equality with the Father but did not cling to it (Philippians 2:6).

Jesus also demonstrated how to honor authority and confront it: Jesus said to them, "Pay to Caesar the things that are Caesars and to God what is God's" (Mark 12:17). Jesus, a Jew, obeyed Caesar as the authority responsible for peace and order. Yet in John 19:11, Jesus answered Pilate by saying: "You would have no authority over me if it were not given to you from above." Jesus, chained and beaten, leveled with Pilate as a person who occupied the authority position. However, He still proclaimed His Father as the supreme source of authority.

The Disparity Lens

As we increase in power and experience, we come from under our parents' authority to become level with them and others. However, if we fail to level with others, we relate to them through a *disparity lens*.

Through the lens of disparity, we consider others as beneath us and don't respect their equality and worth. We may belittle, dismiss, or advise them. We apply double standards to our relationships with them. We consider their needs as not important, while emphasizing what we want from them to meet our needs.

Conversely, through the disparity lens, we also appoint others to be executors of our life. We relegate our authority to them. We seek their permission to fulfill our legitimate responsibilities. We consider their opinions as laws to abide by. We grovel and apologize to them with and without reason.

Through the disparity lens, we equate authority with unquestioning figures. We enthrone those figures high up and don't disagree with them. We blindly follow their decrees and don't recognize the limits of their authority.

Relating through the disparity lens cripples our ability to listen. We don't give speakers equal time or attention. We do not treasure them or make room to receive their views and emotions. Dialogue is possible between equals and is therefore not afforded by disparity. Lastly, disparity triggers conflict with others. It denies others' worthy demands and refuses to afford them equal freedoms.

Luke 18:11 gives a vivid example of relating from the attitude described above in the story of the Pharisee and tax collector. "The Pharisee took his stand ostentatiously and began to pray thus before and with himself: God, I thank You that I am not like the rest of men—extortioners, swindlers, adulterers—or even like this tax collector here." Jesus said that such an attitude caused him to go unjustified.

On the other hand, in Mark 10:46, we read about Bartimaeus, the blind man who lived relating to others from below by begging. However, his faith in Jesus prompted him to correct his attitude and level with others, who tried to silence him. As a result, Jesus stopped and healed him.

11

Guard Your Heart

A Relationship Is Two-way

"Did you get it on Airbnb or Vrbo?" I asked. Shelby said, "Vrbo!" She proceeded to show us, a couple of coworkers, a picture on her cell phone of a private cottage on a lovely lake. Shelby was eager to go on vacation with her newly met boyfriend. Her excitement filled the air. Shelby was a technician with a bubbly personality. She wore her heart on her sleeves (or scrubs, to be precise!).

Fast forward a couple of weeks, and Shelby pushed her cart slowly down the hallway. During the lunch break, she greeted us with a subdued voice and sighed. She said, "He was terrible at connecting. All he wanted to do was drink and play Xbox. We broke up. I switched seats on the plane on the way home so I wouldn't sit next to him." Shelby's boyfriend (now her ex!) did not bond or connect with her. As a result, their short romance came to an end.

We all need to be loved, heard, understood, and valued. We want to seek provision for those needs of relationally mature individuals. They bond with us and respect us as distinct. They treasure us as unique, given our freedom and equality with them. They must relate to us through sound relational lenses of distinctness, integration, and levelness.

Relationships are bidirectional—one direction allows the provision of needs while the opposite direction carries potential emotional harms like abandonment, rejection, or trials. We need to balance meeting our needs against protecting ourselves from harm. We note that harm is more likely at the beginning and end of relationships.

One day, I asked my son, "How do you protect yourself from emotional harm?" He answered with a youth's confidence, "Dad, I am a boxer! I know how to defend myself." An awkward silence prevailed for a few seconds before we both erupted into laughter.

I shared more that what I meant—strong muscles, self-defense courses, and professional personal guards—don't mitigate emotional risk. The emotional risk stems from relational risk. It is the likelihood of relational events that harm our identity and devalue our worth. The risk is real, albeit intangible.

Predictors of Emotional Harm

So how do we predict emotional risk? In the medical profession, we use the term *risk factor* to determine how the presence of a finding increases the probability of an illness occurring in the future. We similarly can point to the following factors that increase the risk of relational harm:

1. Relational delay

Those who are relationally delayed are oblivious to the risk of destructive relationships. They resemble toddlers who may attempt to touch an electric outlet, unaware of the risk of electric shock. They don' t know how to distinguish as safe those who can bond with them and respect their boundaries. As a result, they also disclose themselves to those who abandon or devalue them.

They relate through distorted lenses. They don't consistently bond with friends and end up in isolation without truthful feedback that exposes their illusions. They are deprived of encour-

agement and solidarity when they suffer losses or disappointments. Through the lens of compliance, they don't express words
of protection. Even when they get harmed, they don't even
express it. They prematurely lavish their trust when they experience others' virtuous side.

2. Improper emotional appraisal

Emotional appraisal of a situation reduces exposure to others'
hurtful reactions. Certain individuals may attach an exorbitant
emotional value to a spiritual belief, political association, or
social attitude. When they perceive a violation of their valued
item, they drown in surging emotions and act harmfully.

It is especially wise to remember that spiritual beliefs hold a
steep emotional price. Others form their spiritual beliefs slowly
and treasure them. They would react strongly, perhaps impulsively, if their beliefs were criticized or violated. Through the
levelness lens, we need to value others' spiritual pilgrimage,
albeit different from ours.

3. Emotional debt

Those who experienced distinctness, realize their emotional
debts and work to cancel them. We call it "zeroing the emotional
counter." However, when others are saddled with emotional debt,
they spill a disproportionate flood of emotions under triggers and
devalue us.

Harmful Relational Events

So what are the emotionally harmful events? We delineated
in earlier chapters that relationships are the primary triggers of
emotions. Harmful events are often relational events.

At all times, we maintain responsibility for opening and closing our boundaries. We need to be deliberate about starting or

ending relationships. When we share our pace, time, or thoughts with others, we commence forming a relationship with them.

1. Abandonment

A healthy relationship mutually meets the emotional needs of both parties. If parties conclude that their needs are not being met, they agree to part ways. In contrast, abandonment is the abrupt dissolution of the relationship without warning or plans. Abandonment is an emotional slap on the face. We feel shocked, grief, and hurt.

Those who have not stored enough love feel terrorized when their partner leaves. Their fear of loneliness makes them fuse with a new companion, so they abandon their current partner. The abandoners' continuous cycle of abandoning one and seeking another leads them to isolation. Abandoners don't bond and won't keep consistent emotional ties with others. They were often abandoned in childhood due to the death or negligence of their caregivers.

We must nurture several trusted friendships to lean on them should we experience abandonment from a certain individual. Abandonment can deal a crushing blow to those not bonded with other friends.

It is harmful and risky to indulge in romance and abandon current friendships. It inflicts harm on our friends and leads us to suffocate the romantic relationship with needs, pushing it to the brink of failure. Friendship is the emotional parachute should the romantic jet crash.

Dan and Riley met at the gym and immediately started dating. Dan stopped spending time with his friends. He thought he had found the other half of his soul. One night, after disagreeing with her, she abruptly left and stopped returning his messages. Dan was puzzled about how she vanished without any warning. He learned from social media she had started dating someone else. Dan drowned in sadness. To add insult to injury, he deeply regretted abandoning his friends.

Proverbs 27:10 cautions us about abandoning friends: "Do not forsake your friend, or a friend of your family, and do not go to your relative's house when disaster strikes you, better a neighbor nearby than a relative far away."

2. Betrayal
When we relate through the distinctness lens, we build trust and share ourselves in relationships. We initiate the trust cycle by distinguishing trustworthy others and granting them some credibility. When they respond by faithfulness, we experience trust with them. Trust is deepened by completing and engaging the cycle more times.

Trust entails risking loss. We risk sharing our thoughts, feelings, or possessions. Trust works when we value others more than the things we risk. At the same time, we want to tolerate the loss should it happen. We deliberately risk what is reasonable, doable, and replaceable.

Betrayal happens when the trusted person acts unfaithfully, causing loss or misuse of the risked item. This is more likely when we trust others who are unreliable, or we give too much credit too soon.

The golden standard that describes the trustworthy is that they say what they do and do what they say. They formed a solid identity and related through the distinctness lens. Their life demonstrates signs of ownership and freedom. We can nurture deep friendships and romantic relationships only with the trustworthy.

Once we sharpen our skills to distinguish the trustworthy, we notice how plentiful they are. Don't complain about cheaters but learn to spot the trustworthy. When we trust, we maintain our responsibility for connecting with the trusted and observe their accountability.

When we relate through the integration lens, we comprehend that even the trustworthy have their flaws. We pause, deepening trust with them when they bow to their vices. We resume trust when they take responsibility for them. We recognize that trust is a continuous process of various depths.

Through the splitting lens, we divide people into two exclusive groups: the trustworthy and the cheaters. We lavish all our trust on the trustworthy and infer wrongfully that we can never trust someone who cheated even once.

When we relate through the levelness lens with others, we respect their equality. We accept the slow process of building trust with them. But through the disparity lens, we demand swift and absolute confidence. Such a demand is selfish and offensive.

Jesus loved everyone but trusted only some: "But Jesus did not trust himself to them, because he knew all. He did not need anyone to bear witness concerning man, for he knew all men" (John 2:24).

Paul cautioned the Thessalonians to both love and distance themselves from those who offend: "But if anyone refuses to obey what we say in this letter, take note of that person, and do not associate with him, so that he may be ashamed. Do not regard him as an enemy, but admonish and warn him as a brother" (2 Thessalonians 3:14-15).

Walking in love with someone is not equivalent to trusting them. The deceiver lies to push us to charge just about anyone under the pretense of love, but in the process, we would not have guarded our hearts, which weakens our ability to love others.

3. Rejection
Even if we build trust with others before we make a disclo-

sure to them about themselves, there are no guarantees they will treasure our disclosure. When they dismiss or devalue our disclosures, we experience rejection and feel disappointed, hurt, and angry.

When we relate to others through the distinctness lens, we respect their free will to refuse. When we use the devaluation lens, however, we trespass over their free will to change their no to yes.

When we resolve our inner conflict and relate through the integration lens, we no longer confuse the part for the whole; we comprehend that refusing our request is not the same as refusing us as individuals. Such a distinction is impossible if we relate through the splitting lens because we perceive rejection when others refuse our requests. We incur a much more severe emotional toll, even harm.

We must immerse ourselves in multiple friendships so we can withstand rejection. The harm of rejection is exponentially worse for those who are isolated. Our friends' love, encouragement, and empathy offset the impact of a rejection and help us handle refusals better.

When we walk in love, we treasure others before refusing their requests, thereby reducing the emotional invoice of our refusal. At the same time, we need to speak the truth and say no clearly to irresponsible and selfish requests. A loving no is better than a compliant yes.

Jesus is no stranger to rejection. In Luke 4:16, He went to Nazareth and read the Scripture from Isaiah, prophesying about the Spirit of the Lord on Him. He told the audience, "Today, this scripture is fulfilled in your hearing" (Luke 4:21).

His hometown people, however, rejected His lordship. Jesus quite likely felt frustration, but He respected their freedom to accept or reject His lordship. We observe that He did not argue or attempt to convince them. He leaned on His Father's love and took the good news of His lordship to Judea's surrounding areas.

This begs the following question: Can we spot others who are relationally risky? If so, it will help us set expectations and perhaps avoid harmful relational blunders.

12

Relational Harm

"What is this raucousness all about?" I asked a fellow in the spinning class. He replied with a smirk, "Someone is airdropping his girlfriend's nudes to everyone in the class."

As I adjusted my bike seat, I thought to myself, *What kind of person would scatter the rated M details of a partner who had trusted him?* I felt a mix of sadness and anger. It would be fair to characterize them as relationally risky.

Relationally risky, others are often relationally delayed. They approach others through deformed relational lenses, like devaluation, compliance, splitting, or disparity lenses. They often repeat the same pattern of emotional harm to others and themselves.

The Harm of Deformed Relational Lenses

Relational reality consists of the sum of the relational experiences of the parties involved. Their partner can perceive rejection and withdraw, causing them to experience abandonment. Proverbs 27:14 clearly states, "If anyone loudly blesses their neighbor early in the morning, it will be taken as a curse." Our interaction can be perceived differently by others.

1. The Abandonment Lens

If we don't store enough love perceptions, we don't experience our beloved state when alone. This is the result of abandonment, neglect, or abuse. As a result, we feel extremely lonely and fearful when our partners leave our physical presence. We react by seeking a new partner and abandoning the partner who left.

As abandoners, we make short relationships devoid of meaningful exchanges of thoughts or emotions. We struggle with depression, fear of loneliness, feelings of emptiness, and addictions. Spiritually, abandoners assume God and fellow believers have left them due to sin. They cut themselves from the vine. Jesus said in John 15:5, "I am the vine. You are the branches. If you remain in me and I in you, you will bear much fruit; apart from me, you can do nothing."

We need to receive love perceptions for an extended time until we bond with others. It is wise to postpone romantic relationships until we learn to relate through the distinctness lens and build trust with others.

2. The Devaluation Lens

After we bond with our caregivers, we embark on a journey of discovering our boundaries and our distinct state.

The distinctness lens enables us to perceive others as separate from us. We respect their freedom and responsibility for what is within their boundaries. If we stay fused with our caregiver, we do not relate through the distinctness lens and approach others as an extension of ourselves. This approach devalues others.

Through the devaluation lens, we reduce others to things. We use them to get what we want. We especially do not accept others' no as an answer and attempt to change it to yes. We perceive their freedoms as a threat and engage in arguments and strife.

Through the devaluation lens, we don't lend compassion to others but intimidate them with shouting, insulting, and in some cases, commit physical or sexual violence against them.

We may devalue others in subtle ways too. We lure them into doing what we want, exploiting their needs and weaknesses. We may dangle the false responsibility to trigger their guilt and steer them to comply.

Scripture warns against strife: "Let nothing be done through strife or vainglory, but in lowliness of mind, let each esteem the other better than themselves" (Philippians 2:3).

We need to learn how to confront those who relate through the devaluation lens. We start by affirming their value before refusing their acts of devaluation. We conclude by inviting them to act responsibly. In John 18:23, Jesus confronted the soldier who slapped Him: "If I said something wrong," Jesus replied, "testify as to what is wrong. But if I spoke the truth, why did you strike me?"

If others persist in devaluing us, we must distance ourselves from their presence (2 Thessalonians 3:15). This helps them experience our absence and helps us preserve our character from their lousy company. First Corinthians 15:33 says, "Bad company corrupts good character." We need trustworthy friendships to lean on as we distance ourselves from devaluation.

If devaluation takes the form of violence, we must leave immediately to a safe place and enlist others like law enforcement for help. We need deliberation and patience before pursuing legal proceedings. Such proceedings can be emotionally and financially costly, but at the same time, may bring others to face their distorted ways of relating. We should invite responsibility, not punishment.

Confronting subtle devaluation is tricky. Manipulators skillfully hide their intentions and apologize if confronted. We want to inspect their apologies in light of their readiness to take responsibility for their actions. It may be appropriate to give them less time and shield our intentions from them.

When we relate to God through the devaluation lens, we approach God as a magic wand that gets us the things we want. We don't love God as Jesus described in Matthew 22:37: "Love the Lord with your God with all your heart, and with all your soul, and with all your mind." God delights when we love Him for who He is, not what He gives.

3. The Compliance Lens

Jesus said, "All you need to say is simply 'Yes' or 'No'; anything beyond this comes from the evil one" (Matthew 5:37). Jesus is genuine. His yes means total agreement and His no is a firm refusal. He does not say yes to hide His no.

In contrast, when we don't form an identity, we relate through the compliance lens. We say yes begrudgingly because we fear saying a clear no in order to guard our hearts or disagree.

Through the compliance lens, we open ourselves indiscriminately to others. We melt with them and eventually conform to resemble them. We agree to their requests, even if it is harmful. With no identity, we resemble chameleons who change colors. Romans 12:2 warns about conformity: "Do not conform to the pattern of this world, but be transformed by the renewing of your mind. Then you can test and approve what God's will is—his good, pleasing and perfect will."

Through the compliance lens, we avoid confronting and instead agree falsely. When we do this we hoard scorn and contempt and drown in exhaustion.

We permit irresponsible others into our lives, hoping to secure their love by owning their responsibility. Nevertheless, our attempts to buy love fails, and we perceive ourselves as victims, then lash out at our love subjects!

Through the compliance lens, we act like the fools who feel angry at God for not removing the results of their compulsive agreements: "The foolishness of man subvert his way; Then his heart is resentful and frets against the Lord" (Proverbs 19:3 AMP). God honors our freedom and doesn't rescue us from our choices. It is His way of helping us grow!

4. The Splitting Lens

In John 3:2, Nicodemus, a Jewish ruler, came at night to Jesus, seeking to know the kingdom of God. He was the council member who taught the law during the day but at night was lost and hungry for the kingdom. I always admired Nicodemus' willingness to pursue the kingdom, yet I used to wonder why he was doing it secretly.

Nicodemus hides his doubt lest the counsel condemns him. He is not genuine but splits himself into two—one life in public and the other in secret. Similarly, If we don't receive grace for our flaws, we store them in separate compartments from the good and relate through the splitting lens.

Through the splitting lens, we perceive others as either purely good or disturbingly bad. We focus on others' shortcomings and overlook their many virtues. We are in strife about trivial things and lose focus on what is important. We pursue perfection and end up lonely and disappointed.

As splitters, we feel tainted. We believe that if we disclose our flaws, we will be met with condemnation. We forget that "there is no condemnation for those in Christ" (Romans 8:1). We build walls to hide behind them, but they deprive us of love, hearing, and empathy. We live a life of emotional drought.

Approaching God through the splitting lens, we experience His power on Sunday. But when we leave the church and go back to our lives, we feel powerless and falter in the face of our strongholds.

God desires us to be authentic—that is, the same loving,

overcoming servants day or night, weekend or weekday. He administers His grace tirelessly to roll away our shame. We need to speak truthfully about our flaws (Ephesians 4:15) and receive grace from God and gracious saints. We then can stop hiding our shortcomings from others and detesting them in others.

Paul was a violent prosecutor for the church, but he told Timothy in his first letter: "The grace of our God was poured on me abundantly along with the faith and love that are in Christ Jesus" (v.14). He became the one who rejoiced in being poured out as a drink on the sacrifice of the saints.

5. The Disparity Lens:

When we don't level with others, we do not approach them as equal and worthy. We relate to them vertically through the disparity lens. We either enthrone ourselves as their guardians or act like their children.

In relating vertically with others, we advise them with or without an invitation. Our advice reeks of mocking, ridiculing, and belittling. We don't hold others equal to us in responsibility and freedom. We make them accountable to the highest standards but find a way to give ourselves exceptions that stir conflicts.

We play the father figure in friendship and romance. We end those relationships as soon as our partners seek equality.

Conversely, through the disparity lens, we idolize others with fame, knowledge, or experience. We inaugurate them as rulers over us and do not question their choices. We grovel before them and avoid independent decisions, awaiting their final approval.

I am not discarding the idea of Christian mentors who come along to guide us in our journey of growth. Paul asked the Corinthians to imitate him (1 Corinthians 41:6). But we level with those who are guiding us and recognize them as people who occupy the position of mentorship. We submit to their role in freedom to receive truthfulness and grace. We can disagree with their irresponsible or unjust guidance. We also stay responsible for ourselves.

Paul told Timothy in 1 Timothy 4:12, "Do not let anyone look down on you, because you are young, but set an example for the believers in speech in conduct in faith in love and impurity." The message is clear— when you put yourself at an equal level with others, you grow in love and faith.

Let us not look down on others due to our act of service or spiritual talent. Jesus says in Matthew 23:11, "The greatest among you will be your servant." Jesus sees serving others as the highest order in His kingdom.

In conclusion, those who relate through deformed relational lenses will likely harm others and ignite conflicts with them. To complicate matters, these distorted lenses skew our perception of God's character.

We should not react to relational risk by isolating ourselves. We need to walk in love and relate to others through the distinctness, integration, and levelness lenses. This is how we shine the lights for others. Matthew 5:1 says, "Let your light shine before men so that they may see your good deeds and moral excellence and glorify your father who is in heaven."

Shining the light, however, will take additional relational steps of listening, forgiving, and managing conflict. This brings us to the exciting topic of listening to others. I invite you to join me.

13

Listening as a Love Language

Why Does Listening Matter?

It is a warm afternoon in September. I phoned my brother Sam to discuss our dad's health. We traded the usual exchange of pleasantries, then I said I wanted to talk about Dad's hearing problem.

Sam's muffled answer was punctured by a young girl screaming, "Daddy, I lost it!" A nearby TV (I assumed) then blasted a volley of advertisements.

I pressed the phone closer to my sweaty ear. Raising my voice a bit to drown out the noise, I said, "Dad's hearing has worsened. I think he needs to see an audiologist."

This time, Sam interrupted me and said, "I am sorry. The girls are asking me to retrieve their tennis balls. It fell in the neighbor's backyard."

The issue with our dad's hearing is not urgent, but I still hoped to be heard and understood. A wave of frustration engulfed me. Realizing the situation's futility, I composed my voice and politely said, "Let's schedule another call so we can bounce thoughts."

The story is common. We need to be listened to and understood. This need is relational, meaning we can meet it in relationships with others. Knowing that we are listened to entices us to introduce ourselves more and feel cared for. Listeners, on their end, need to hear our words and receive our thoughts and feelings.

Listening makes it possible to exchange appreciation and honor with our loved ones. It is through such exchanges that we experience our self-worth and help others claim theirs. This is more important than ever in today's world, where people pursue professional or financial success as a means to achieve worth.

On a spiritual level, listening to God's Word helps us know His character better and appreciate His faithfulness. According to Romans 10:17, "Consequently faith comes from hearing the message and then messages heard through the word about Christ."

1. Listening Wholeheartedly

Wholehearted listening is more than hearing spoken words. It means receiving the speakers as whole individuals with their thoughts and feelings. As wholehearted listeners, we want to free enough room in ourselves to receive the speaker's thoughts and feelings. The key to freeing the needed room is saying no to false responsibilities and meddling. Paul said in 2 Thessalonians 3:11, "Indeed, we hear that some among you are disorderly being busy with other people's affairs, instead of their own, and doing no work."

The toll of past relational injuries can flood all the emotional rooms in our hearts, leaving no room for empathy. We need to acknowledge our current responses and heal from those injuries to vacate the necessary space for empathy with others.

Our empathy and truthfulness helps others renew their perceptions of past injuries and makes them feel more loved and less hurt. Proverbs 27:9 says, "Oil and perfume rejoice the heart, so does the sweetness of friends' counsel that comes from the heart." Listening does not change injuries but changes our current perceptions of them and therefore eases the emotional pain.

When we speak, we produce verbal and nonverbal content. The verbal content is our spoken words, while the nonverbal manifests in our vocal inflections and facial expressions. Before we express ourselves verbally, we need to acknowledge our emotions, so we can align our verbal and nonverbal content together. We can employ our emotions in passionate expressions when our tone and expressions match the meanings of our spoken words. Many online speakers coach their audience to become more influential by mastering their speech inflections, but they neglect the emotional healing that underpins such ability.

When we fail to align our verbal and nonverbal expressions, listeners receive our nonverbal before we decode our words.

I watched a podcast speaker expressing his views about a person accused of a disgraceful act. The speaker repeated how much he respected the accused offender, but I couldn't help but notice his loud voice and furrowed eyebrows. The speaker, at one point, removed any doubt about his intentions by telling the would-be offender, "If you could see yourself in the mirror, you would vomit!" Viewers' comments confirmed what I sensed all along: the speaker's expression was insulting.

2. Listening and Loving

We can listen to others only if we pause what we say or do. In granting others our time and undivided attention, we show that we care about them. As they speak and we listen to them, we have an opportunity to affirm their worth. We need to focus on receiving them as a whole and defer giving our opinions. Proverb 18:2 says, "A fool has no delight in understanding but only in revealing his personal opinions and himself."

When we relate with others through the integration lens, we treasure them as unique despite our differences with them. We recognize that they are much more than their views.

Through the levelness lens, we perceive others as worthy of being listened to, regardless of their title or reputation. We offer them equal time to express themselves and don't borrow their time to speak.

Love motivates us to speak the truth (Ephesians 4:15). We honor others and offer empathy and understanding before giving truthful feedback. This way, our affirmation supports them so they can withstand our input.

We express our truthfulness humbly. We are cognizant that speakers too have their truthful perceptions. Once both of us share truthfulness, a more complete truth emerges. The relational truth can't be subjected to the logic of right and wrong, for it is the sum of the truthful perceptions of the parties. As noted earlier, Proverbs 27:14 describes a person who greets another early in the morning, but that person perceives it as a curse.

Finally, in listening, we celebrate speakers' achievements. We celebrate the achiever first and then the achievements. Each listening round is a miniature celebration.

3. Responsible Listening

When we experience our distinctness from our caregivers, We begin hearing our thoughts and distinguishing our feelings. We become acquainted with ourselves and more able to listen to others. When we listen to expressions, our listening increases in responsibility, from listening to clichés and gossip to listening to thoughts and emotions.

A cliché is a statement to kill time more than convey self. For example, my colleague enters our workplace, an intensive care unit, and tells everyone, "Are we in business today?" He does not seek a meaningful answer.

Gossip is done by those who have not experienced distinctness and don't effectively express themselves. They fill the resulting void with gossip, which doesn't help us know them as individuals.

Salma is a coworker with a bubbly personality. She comes to the lunch room during her break to gossip about others. She inhales her food and simultaneously tells about her girlfriend's party. She criticizes the woman's outfit but praises her fiancé for his stylish blazer.

We want to honor those who gossip and yet state our intentions not to listen. Similarly, we shouldn't pay attention or listen to gossip on social media and TV. Indeed, the power of social media speakers comes from those who grant listening and empower speakers.

Proverbs 16:28 says. "A perverse person stirs up conflict, and gossip separates close friends." Love doesn't harm: "Love does not harm a neighbor. Therefore, love is the fulfillment of the law" (Romans 13:10). Love, therefore, doesn't participate in gossip. In the lunchroom, I found it helpful to remove myself from the situation or put on my headphones.

In contrast to gossip, listening to expressions of thought helps us know speakers and offer our understanding. Consider this real-life story:

> Joshua enters his humble studio after a day of work at the vineyard. He washes his tanned face and sits at the simple dining table. He tells his wife, "Today I thought about what would happen if I lost my job. I want to buy disability insurance."

> His wife nods her head with gratitude and says, "Tell me more."

When we listen to others expressing their thoughts, we know the type of people they are. Because their thoughts are the seeds that germinate their words and choices, listening to others' intentions can deepen trust with them. If their intentions are not clear, it is prudent to ask them to verbalize them. We aim to clarify misunderstandings and prevent injustice.

God desires to disclose His thoughts. As soon as we are born again, the Holy Spirit begins conveying His thoughts to us. They are thoughts of honor, purity, and righteousness. "Finally brothers and sisters, whatever is true, whatever is noble, whatever is right, whatever is pure, whatever is lovely, whatever is admirable—if there is excellent or praiseworthy, think about such things" (Philippians 4:8).

We must take the time to listen to the Holy Spirit's thoughts. As we agree with them, we displace our deformed perceptions and shed the deformed relational lenses. His thoughts help us examine our motives. Hebrews 4:12 says, "For the word of God is alive and active. Sharper than any double-edged sword, it penetrates even to dividing soul and spirit, joints and marrow; it judges the thoughts and attitudes of the heart." And the Word of God renews our minds (Romans 12:2).

When others share their thoughts, we know their type. But, when they share their emotions, we know the real story. Their feelings are unique to them and reflect their perceptions and experiences. Perhaps the most responsible listening is when we hear about expressions of emotions. It is a powerful way to give empathy and care.

Mark oversees a maternity department in a local hospital. He has worked hard on improving services, yet recently the department saw a surge in dissatisfied patients. The board of trustees asks for a meeting to discuss the issue. Mark asks his trustworthy friend for a listening session so that he can verbalize his sadness and frustration. This way, he will express his feelings before attending the meeting.

We need to welcome listening to loved ones desiring to express their emotions. But we need to plan listening sessions and discourage them from hit-and-run venting. We must refuse false responsibility in our busy lives so we can free more time for listening sessions. Such listening sessions should be face-to-face, so we observe the speaker's nonverbal content and receive their emotions. This, in turn, helps them to control themselves and steers them away from acting impulsively.

We shouldn't enable accusations or condemnation against others, but we need to focus on offering our understanding, empathy, and if appropriate, truthful feedback.

Speakers who don't align their verbal and non-verbal expressions have stored many emotions. We will likely receive their nonverbal messages before we decipher their spoken facts. We need to use insight and logic to understand their expressions.

Inevitably, listening to the Holy Spirit is the pinnacle of listening. Keep in mind that He speaks through our fellow saints. We want to give this listening our utmost attention.

The Holy Spirit expresses His thoughts and plans for each individual. He informs us that we are loved, protected, and cared for: "For I know the plans I have for you declares the Lord plans to prosper you, and not to harm you plans to give you hope and future" (Jeremiah 29:11).

The Holy Spirit is all-knowing and does not need to ask questions to gather information. He rarely asks questions. Whatever messages He conveys to you, it is meant for you individually. Do not try to deflect it to others. Yes, some prophets speak messages to others, but we carry God's presence within us and have direct access to Him. Listening to saints will help us confirm. Hallelujah.

Jesus emphasized the importance of listening. He often concluded parables by telling the crowd, "He who has ears to hear, let them hear" (Mark 4:9). Let's pause our doing so we can listen to the Holy Spirit's words. Revelation 2:29 says, "He who can hear, let listen to and heed what the Spirit says to the assemblies." His words are life and life-giving.

14

Relational Listening

Listen to Yourself!

I have always despised silence since I was a kid. Yet, years ago, during a northeast blizzard (Nor'easter!), the silence was all I had. Here's a little context. Having come out of failed relationships, I had taken a break from work. Back then, I had not nurtured deep friendships. I leaned (throwing myself would be a better term!) on God for answers.

Amid the silence. I started to hear my contradictory perceptions. My heart was throbbing with hurt and sadness. Finding it hard to fall asleep, I grabbed my tablet and began to journal my thoughts and feelings. It was initially awkward to do, but the Holy Spirit whispered to me, "You can do all things with Me." Soon, my shame and hurt started to fade.

Fast forward to the present, I am reviewing my journal. It is interesting to reflect on how distorted my thoughts were back then. They were biased against me and others. What an amazing testimony of God's grace and guidance that led me to renew my mind.

When we store enough love perceptions, we experience being loved while alone. We move away from our parents to affirm our boundaries and recognize our distinct states. As we experience distinctness, we get our first glimpse of ourselves. We consider the thoughts occupying our minds. We feel our emotions and observe our bodies experiencing their energy.

Taking an inventory of thoughts is the first step toward responsibility for them. We trace many thoughts to listening to our parents, while we trace others to our interactions with friends, reading books, or watching media. Our constructed ways of understanding relationships become our relational lenses or attitudes.

What we listen to becomes part of our thought inventory. Therefore, we must carefully select the speakers and the content to listen to. We should not listen to what is hateful, irresponsible, or unjust. David describes the state of his thoughts in Psalm 55:3: "My thoughts trouble me, and I am distraught because of what my enemy is saying, because of the threats of the wicked. They bring down suffering on me, and I assail me in their anger."

My retired friend Shirley complained about how much hostile rhetoric she is forced to listen to on television. We prayed together over the issue. After a few days, she confided in me and said, "God told me to restrict my time watching television." She started filling that time by visiting hospices and archiving her family pictures. She and I still laugh at how simple and effective God's solution was.

Television's threats to our thoughts are insignificant compared to social media. Social media outlets relentlessly export their reactions and assumptions. If we are not careful, those virtual assumptions slowly displace our love and truthfulness perceptions.

It is not a mystery. What we give our time to think about becomes an idol that turns us away from God. Jonah 2:8 says, "Those who cling to worthless idols turn away from God's love for them." That is why we want to scrutinize our thought life. We need to prioritize time for fellowship with the Holy Spirit and reading the Word. The Holy Spirit credits those words to our minds as love, power, and wisdom perceptions. We need to keep the throne of our thought life for God.

Owning our emotions helps us become better listeners. We must forgive those who offended us and cancel their emotional indebtedness to us. This enables us to manage our emotions while listening to speakers who sound or look like our offenders. We will get better at giving empathy to speakers.

Listening and Relational Lenses

Our relational lens toward others dictates how we perceive them and feel about them. This is especially true when we listen to speakers, for the relational lens we use to approach them influences our listening to them.

If we relate to speakers through the devaluation lens, we dismiss the importance of their opinions or beliefs. We do not afford them our attention or empathy. We don't notice their non-verbal expressions and may write them off as individuals.

When we relate with speakers through the integration lens, we reconcile their verbal and nonverbal expressions. We don't selectively receive the speakers' nonverbal expressions and miss the meaning of their words. We receive their message despite the distracting details. Integration cancels selective hearing!

If we relate to speakers through the splitting lens, we will likely be impacted by their expressions in ways different from what they had intended. Again, Proverbs 27:14 says, "If anyone loudly blesses their neighbor early in the morning, it will be taken as a curse." The blessing intended was experienced by the neighbor due to the loud voice in the early morning.

Furthermore, we may attach meanings to their spoken words that differ from those they attach to them. We can clarify how their expressions impact us.

At the end of my shift one day, an incoming colleague said, "Good morning, professor!" I felt annoyed and told him that I did not appreciate the word. He apologized and elaborated that he used the word as a compliment. It is always better to ask for clarification of expressions.

In relating through the levelness lens, we perceive speakers as worthy and equal. We comprehend how they, like us, deserve to be listened to and understood. Yet, they are unique in how they express and meet those needs. We allow them to share their beliefs without perceiving them as a threat. We enable their attempts to persuade us and may even adopt some of their loving, responsible views.

In John 4:1-29, the disciples were surprised to find Jesus talking with a Samaritan woman. But Jesus spoke, listened, and leveled with her. As a result, she was adopted into the kingdom and testified to her town.

The Listening Session

Listening is loving. It is a deliberate caring and giving effort. It is not different from buying a gift for someone we adore. We brainstorm ideas for gifts and research them online. When it comes to listening, we too need to set the stage for the listening session before we give it.

Planning for the session requires the following steps in this particular order:

1. Presence

Physical face-to-face presence is best for the listening session. We can invite speakers to a safe place or solicit their input for choosing a location. The place can be private or public, but the latter is more suited for speakers with whom we have not built trust. Outdoor walks are a great option.

In this age of technology, presence means we make ourselves reachable on our devices so speakers can message or talk with us. With virtual presence, we can acknowledge receiving the communication and respond by planning a listening session.

We should not equate presence with listening, as listening needs ample time and emotional room. So it is preferred not to schedule listening sessions late at night in order to receive speakers with their thoughts and emotions. We certainly should not engage in random listening sessions.

2. Attention

Attention follows presence. We focus on the meanings of the speakers' spoken words and observe their nonverbal expressions, such as their vocal inflections and facial expressions.

Giving undivided attention dictates that we pause talking when the speaker expresses their thoughts. We postpone any tasks, especially glancing at cell phones or television. By pausing, we declare to speakers that they matter the most to us at the current moment. For families with kids, giving attention requires getting help with kids to prevent distractions.

Jesus made Himself present to the Father early before others needed His attention: "Very early in the morning while it was still dark, Jesus got up and left the house and went off to solitary place when he prayed" (Mark 1:35).

3. Empathy

We have to reject the guilt of false responsibilities, so we vacate the emotional room to host the speaker's emotions. This is how we sympathize with speakers. But with empathy, we come close to feeling what speakers feel. When we empathize with speakers, we help them examine their expressed perceptions. It is a fantastic revelation about the power of listening.

We must forgive those who violated us and write off their emotional debts. Festered offense resembles an emotional ticking bomb. Upon hearing certain words or names, it detonates and produces a flood of feelings, leaving no room for empathy.

4. Encouragement

We want to enable the flow of thoughts and emotions from the speaker. Therefore, we won't interrupt speakers or assess their views. We want to listen to speakers' journey to their current beliefs. One of the ways to honor speakers is by offering appreciation and understanding for their journey.

An excellent strategy is to postpone questions until the latter part of the listening sessions. We also won't pivot the conversation to be around us, which is selfish and uncaring.

Sound relational lenses help facilitate the flow. Through the bonding lens, we don't abandon the listening session. Being rooted in love qualifies us to perceive our state of being beloved and resign our inner judge. We then can restrain ourselves from judging speakers. When we judge speakers, we declare our lack of interest in them and discourage more expressions. Very little flow (if ever) occurs after judgment.

Through the distinctness lens, we stay calm inside our boundaries when speakers become too animated. The Scripture notes that staying calm frustrates the enemy and declares our victory: "without being frightened in any way by those who oppose you. This is a sign to them that they will be destroyed, but that you will be saved—and that by God" (Philippians 1:28).

When we relate through the integration lens, we do not perceive speakers' anger as an attack. Instead, we comprehend that it reflects their demands, whether worthy or not!

Through the levelness lens, we offer speakers equal time to express themselves. We do not usurp time but encourage them to use their half.

5. Feedback

Once we receive speakers with their thoughts and feelings, we reach a point where we can respond. Our response starts with honoring speakers before giving them feedback. Honoring speakers will help them withstand our candid feedback.

We wrap our feedback with kindness before verbalizing it. We have owned our emotions and are therefore able to reign our nonverbal cues. We verbalize our truthfulness to the speakers, focusing on their actions, not character.

In listening to the speaker's journey, we are better equipped to offer an understanding of their intentions and actions.

We need to give our feedback in small amounts, just enough required to clarify our views. Extensive feedback can be perceived as venting, which burdens the speaker and devalues them. This threatens to nullify the care that listening is supposed to provide.

In the unique case of grief, very little feedback is needed. Instead, we want to be present with those who grieve without rationalizing, preaching, or attempting to change the mood to cheerful.

Love invites hope and responsibility. Our feedback should invite speakers to accept responsibility. In John 5:8, Jesus listens to the paralyzed man by the pool of Bethesda, giving truthful, caring, and brief feedback: "Get up! Pick up your mat and walk."

God creates, heals, and forgives with His Word. He longs to express Himself to us through His Word. Let's set the stage for listening to Him. On the other hand, the Holy Spirit attempts to interrupt us daily; we need to pause and obey the soft voice!

Psalm 46:10 says, "Be still and know that I am God." It is simple yet elusive for some. We won't know the Holy Spirit until we pause. Prayers are not monologues of requesting and petitioning. Those who pause are the ones who get most intimate with God.

Our listening to the Holy Spirit should be wholehearted. His words inform us about the glory of Jesus, and His emotions reveal His righteous and just thoughts. Listening to God is the venue for us to receive His influence, grace, and favor.

15

Dialogue and Disclose

Level to Dialogue

"Are you invited?" my friend, Sam, asked.

"No," I said, with a chuckle.

"It is lavish. Full menu, elegant place," said Sam.

"I hope they have fun. I am not a fan of lavish parties for baptisms or other occasions."

"Can I share something with you about this town? I grew up here. Ordinary people hold big parties."

"Thank you," I said. "I respect their traditions, but I believe they can put their income to use for other pressing needs. The baptism can be celebrated with affordable accommodations."

"Good point," said Sam. "At the same time, the way I see it, life in this town tends to be somewhat dull. Locals celebrate to experience joy."

"It is a thoughtful perspective. One of the languages of love is gifts. The gift may as well be a party."

Sam nodded at my comments.

"I thank you, Sam. I feel enriched by this exchange."

"Likewise," my friend said.

Previously, we recognized the importance of wholehearted listening. We want to make room to receive the speaker's thoughts and emotions. When speakers and listeners level with each other, the flow of thoughts and emotions is maximized between them. This is the birth of dialogue.

The speaker symbolizes levelness in dialogue by using the pronoun *I* to define him or herself. It removes the speaker's titles and seats them evenly with listeners. The word *I* emphasizes responsibility for the words spoken, emotions felt, and attitude adopted. In contrast, using the pronoun *we* in dialogue lumps speakers and listeners together, and it obliterates the lines of responsibility.

Relating through the levelness lens enables equality. We are entitled to an equal share of time. We, as speakers, purposely use our quota of time to argue our views. We won't borrow time from the listeners but encourage them to use their share of the time.

Equality in dialogue extends to personal responsibility. Speakers and listeners are equally responsible for staying connected. Both continue the work until we reach mutual enrichment. We won't abandon the dialogue suddenly.

Speakers and listeners have equal presence in dialogue. We relate to listeners in their present state. We don't relate to their image formed from assumptions, fame, or memories. In contrast, if they attempt to dialogue with our old image, we will affirm our current views. We won't align our responses to match their perceptions.

Dialogue is the peak of listening and expressing. Both parties uncover each other's dreams, convictions, and demands. Both get enriched, treasured, and celebrated.

The following may jolt many, but God is open to us arguing our grievances with and demands of Him: "Review the past for me, let us argue the matter together, state the case for your innocence" (Isaiah 43:26). It is a fantastic display of His humility, kindness, and justice. Throughout the dialogue with Him, we ascribe to Him the honor, reverence, and thankfulness He deserves.

The Trustworthy

Sitting in my seat, I saw a petite woman walking the narrow corridor between the airplane seats. She looked intently at the row numbers. She breathed a sigh of relief as she located her row. She sat by another man and me.

As the flight attendants demonstrated safety procedures, the male passenger quipped that it was boring. He turned to the petite woman and asked, "Are you nervous about flying?"

"Yes, a little!" she said. "This is only my first flight. I prefer to travel by car."

"By the way, I am Bill."

"Layla."

"I own my business!" said Bill. "What do you do for a living?"

Layla said, "I substitute at an elementary school."

They conversed more while I took an acrobatic position to attempt to sleep in the tight seat (I fly economy!).

Sleeping in an airplane seat is not my forte. All I know is that I heard Bill saying: "Let's grab a drink after landing and head to my studio!"

This real-life story shows how some open themselves to others they meet accidentally. They do not examine others' credibility nor take the time to build trust. They don't recognize the risk of self-disclosure.

We do not take medication without consulting medical professionals (or Google!) about the effects. Yet, forming emotional ties with others is not different from taking a drug. When we let others in, we permit inside us some of their fears, demands, and hopes. First Corinthians 15:33 says, "Bad company ruins good character." Giving or receiving disclosure requires the utmost attention and deliberation.

In experiencing distinctness, we become conscious of ourselves. In our conquest to be loved, we ponder revealing ourselves to others. Nonetheless, we fear if they see the real us, they may respond with dismissal or ridicule.

It is not a question of whether we need to disclose ourselves; instead, can we build trust with the recipients before our disclosure? The first and most vital step in building trust is distinguishing trustworthy people. Those must be rooted in love and able to relate through the bonding lens. We don't want the disappointment of attempting to build trust with someone only to find that they have abandoned the relationship.

The trustworthy use their no to clarify their principles and safeguard their heart. They refuse irresponsibility and speak truthfully. They are free from the false responsibility of fixing others emotionally and are not afraid of avoiding disagreeing with others.

Through the distinctness lens, the trustworthy respect our freedom and personal responsibility. They declare their intentions and consistently act according to their beliefs. They say what they do and do what they say, and there are no gaps between their words and deeds. Proverbs 25:14 says, "Like clouds and wind, without rain is one who boasts of gifts never given."

There is an old saying: Fortune favors the brave. To that, we can add, love favors the trustworthy. We must activate the trust cycle with the trustworthy to pursue love with them.

After choosing reliable candidates, we take the initiative by interacting with them. Taking the initiative dictates that we treasure others through the distinctness lens. We also need to overcome the fear of rejection and the shame of being exposed. Those who relate through the compliance lens do not take the initiative but wait for others to make the first move.

Interacting with others isn't equivalent to disclosing ourselves. We reveal our beliefs, attitudes, and feelings later once trust is deepened. Once we have made the connection, we give others limited credibility and take some risks with them. Lending credibility means we willfully assume they have goodwill and will do as they say.

Taking risks with others has different forms—we disclose our thoughts or feelings about them or risk money or possessions in business ventures. The risk we take is reasonable. We risk what is responsible, doable, or achievable. For example, you can risk introducing yourself to someone you often see at your local church or gym. It is attainable that they will reciprocate.

On the other hand, if you want to bet all your savings on a single stock, it would be best if you comprehended that the risk is unreasonable. It is up to how much loss you can responsibly tolerate or recover.

When trusted candidates respond to our initiative by executing as they said, we experience their reliability. The trust cycle is completed.

The trust cycle is dynamic; it deepens when we take more risks and experience additional credibility. In Luke 16:10, Jesus told the disciples, "Whoever can be trusted with very little can also be trusted with much, and whoever is dishonest with very little will also be dishonest with much."

Deepening trust is deliberate; we pause when the trusted acts irresponsibly. We can categorically withdraw credibility if we observe repeated neglect or violation.

Trust isn't an excuse to abandon connecting with the trusted and observing their credible behavior. We also stay connected with other reliable friends to examine reality. Through the levelness lens, we do not demand or beg others to trust us. Trust requires equal parties to toil in the process.

Trust is risky, yet the door leads to the safety of connectedness. If we cower in the face of building trust, we will rot in isolation and drown in despair and illusions.

Self-disclosure

Having deepened trust, we disclose to the trusted our views, beliefs, and memories. We may go further and reveal how we feel about them.

We need to disclose our flaws and injuries to integrated saints. The Holy Spirit directs the recipient saints to dispense grace and truth in words, prayers, and laying on of hands. In receiving grace from them, we reconcile our faulty parts and become authentic. Agreeing with their truthful perceptions helps us renew our perceptions and feelings about injuries. James 5:16 says, "Therefore confess your sins to each other and pray for each other so you may be healed. The prayer of a righteous person is powerful and effective."

Self-disclosure is done freely, not under pressure or promises from listeners. Unreliable people use promises to boost their credibility. In contrast, the trustworthy work patiently so we can experience their credibility and risk disclosing to them. We also avoid impulsive disclosures to roommates, coworkers, or others we meet by coincidence. Similarly, we don't disclose to listeners due to their popularity or achievements.

In disclosing through the distinctness lens, we also maintain ownership of the contents we reveal. We decide when, how, and with whom it can be shared.

Listeners cannot use our disclosure without our permission. We are also responsible for our thoughts and feelings during the disclosure. We don't assume the recipients will correct our illusions or pay our emotional debts.

Sarah and Michael are dating. She discloses to him that her ex-boyfriend had sexually assaulted her. Michael feels angry and contemplates confronting the guy to teach him a lesson. However, after cooling down and praying, he recognizes that would be selfish.

Sarah is responsible for the revealed content and for pursuing her healing. She can confront the aggressor should she choose to. She decides to see a therapist, and Michael supports her by sending a personal card. Proverbs 25:9 says, "Debate your case with your neighbor, and not disclose the secret to another."

We must be mindful of the emotional toll on the wholehearted listeners; they consume their emotional budget in listening to our disclosures. Our disclosure has to be gently done in installments that they can process. We can distribute the disclosure toll by disclosing it to a small group of trustworthy listeners.

It is loving to hold off disclosing if the recipient cannot withstand the emotional burden. Meeting our needs to be healed, loved, and understood must not be done at the expense of harming the listeners.

We want the content disclosed to be verifiable. If possible, we want those involved to be present during disclosure. This helps deter any assumptions of exaggeration.

In conclusion, self-disclosure is essential to experience love and healing. Few plan to live in an emotional drought, yet it is the inevitable end when we fail to disclose ourselves to the trustworthy.

God himself is trustworthy. He does as He says and says what He does. He declares in Matthew 24:35, "Heaven and earth will pass away, but my words will not pass away." His identity has not, does not, and will not change. "Jesus Christ is the same yesterday, today, and forever" (Hebrews 13:8).

This faithful God knew some would reject Him, yet He took a risk by loving everyone first. Those who respond in credibility by loving Him back will experience His faithfulness.

Knowing that God does not put unreasonable demands on us, I have always wondered why it's impossible to please God without faith (Hebrews 11:6). Then it dawned on me: God wants us to experience His character and love Him for who He is, not for the things He gives. We then can love others. First John 4:19 says, "We love because he first loved us."

Once we have faith in God, we experience Jesus' words in Luke 12:23, how life is more than food and body more than clothes.

16

The Love Motive

More than a Feeling!

"Was that love or stupid infatuation?" Ashley asked and tearfully sighed. She was expressing to our small group her anguish over her breakup.

Ashley was introduced to a handsome man with Christian values. The icing was that he coached ice hockey (no pun intended!). They dated for three weeks before going on a romantic getaway in South America. Ashley shared that the trip went well for a day and some. But then it became marred with arguments and assault before it came to a quiet conclusion.

She said with utter confusion: "I fell for him and enjoyed some closeness. He had an ugly side, and it ended up hurting me. I feel ashamed of the whole thing."

We listened intently and praised her courage in sharing that with us. A few of us gathered around her as our leader prayed.

The story is not unusual. The misconceptions regarding love are many. Some equate love with intimacy, and others equate it with being attracted to someone or having a crush. For some disappointed others, love no longer exists. Some engage in irresponsible, even risky conduct to hear the words, "I love you."

We all have an inherent relational need to be loved, heard, and accepted. Our need to be loved probably trumps other relational needs. We feel loved when perceived as valued, cared for, and idolized. Love as a feeling is highly personal, coming from the unique perceptions of the individual.

Scripture tells us that we must walk in love: "This is the commandment, just as you have heard from the beginning, that you should walk in love" (2 John 1:6). And to grow in the knowledge of love: "And this is my prayer: that your love may abound more and more in knowledge and depth of insight so that you may be able to discern what is best and may be pure and blameless for the day of Christ" (Philippians 1:9-11).

When we are youth, we think love is a magical feeling that engulfs us and spices up our dull life. As we grow relationally, we recognize that emotions are products of perceptions. What we call "love" in everyday language is a relationship where perceptions of value, care, and admiration are exchanged.

Our motives lie deep in ourselves and induce our interactions, which then are translated into loving behavior through our relational lenses. Love is a motive, an interaction, and a feeling.

Philippians 2:5 says, "In your relationships with one another, have the same mindset as Christ Jesus." The Holy Spirit helps us align our love motive with that of Jesus. Then through the sound relational lenses, we express the love motive as loving behavior. We aim to discern genuine love relationships and confront the false harmful ones.

The Character of Love Motive

The motives embedded in our character guide our interactions. The love motive manifests through the sound relational lenses into behavior the Bible calls walking in love: "Little children, let's not love with words or speech, but with action and truth" (1 John 3:18).

The Holy Spirit led Paul to describe the moral parameters of the love motive in his first letter to the Corinthians. Love motive is characterized by the following:

1. Love protects

The love motive guide to protecting the beloved in 1 Corinthians 13:7 admonishes us to do no harm. Romans 13:10 says, "Love does no harm to a neighbor."

Through the *distinctness lens*, we do no harm by respecting others' separateness. If we were to protect or honor others, we would cross only the necessary boundaries to avoid shattering their privacy.

Through the distinctness lens, we do no harm to others by declining to own their personal responsibilities. We refrain from reading their mind and speaking for them. We don' t envy them for their successes (1 Corinthians 13:4). We exhort them to bear the results of their choices. It is their path to grow in ownership and freedom.

Doing no harm through the *integration lens* means we don't paint others as evil if we see their defects. We extend grace to them before giving them our truthful feedback.

We omit the use of words that imply belittlement, sarcasm, or insults. Ephesian 4:29 says, "Do not let any unwholesome talk come out of your mouth, but only what helps build others up according to their needs, that it may benefit those who listen."

Frank returns from work and finds out that his dinner is not ready. He feels hungry, and his anger boils. He gives his spouse a death stare and tells her loudly, "You know I love you, but I told you thousands of times that my dinner has to be ready at five o'clock!" Frank's words of love are over-shadowed by his demeaning nonverbal expressions.

2. Love honors

Love prompts us to honor others (1 Corinthians 13:5). We honor others through the levelness lens by treasuring their precious value, which is an inherent value unrelated to their achievements or titles. We affirm their value with words or deeds that convey honor, gratitude, and celebration. When appropriate, we affirm others with gentle physical gestures like shaking hands or patting shoulders. (We want to be mindful of building trust with others before physically touching them.) Honoring others through the levelness lens also means honoring their equality. We do not relate to them as if we are someone from above them (1 Corinthians 13:4).

When conversing with them, we sit at their level, making eye contact and addressing them by name. It is vital to be in control of your emotions before responding to others. Love is not easily angered (1 Corinthians 13:5). We do not bottle negative emotions, lest they spill through our nonverbal expressions and devalue others. We zero our emotional counter so we won't be angered easily.

Honoring others may take the form of giving. We may provide services to help others with their needs. Even better, we can give them gifts to celebrate them as individuals regardless of the occasion.

Kelly gives Janet a check to help with her daughter's surgery expenses for which Janet is grateful. In a few weeks, Janet receives a gift card signed by Kelly, so she can take her recovering daughter to their favorite steakhouse. Janet's tears flowed as she read the note. She felt deeply touched.

3. Love speaks the truth

Love rejoices with the truth (1 Corinthians 13:6). The love motive induces us to be truthful with our words, and even more importantly, our emotions. We want our verbal expressions to inform the beloved what we genuinely feel.

Emotional honesty means relinquishing false cheerfulness. We need to admit our past relational losses and embrace the resulting sadness. In grief, we let go of old perceptions and make room for new ones. We can genuinely laugh in joy only after we have wept in sadness. Ecclesiastes 7:3 AMPC says, "Sorrow is better than laughter, for by the sadness of the countenance the heart is made better and gains gladness." Love rejoices with the joyful and grieves with the sad.

Speaking the truth through the distinctness lens, we say a clear no to false responsibility. We must give up attempts to buy love by sacrificing good deeds. Jesus says in Matthew 9:13, "I desire mercy, not sacrifice."

Speaking the truth through the integration lens, we speak words that bestow grace on others as a whole rather than criticize their shortcomings. Of course, we need to have received grace before we can dispense it to others (2 Corinthians 1:4).

Speaking the truth through the levelness lens means we bring our truthfulness to the beloved, so we can combine it with theirs to construct the complete relational truth. "Love is kind" (1 Corinthians 13:4). Therefore, we drape our honesty with kindness before speaking. Love aims for truthfulness to illuminate others, not tarnish them.

Speaking the truth means we respond with words of thank-fulness when we are honored and don't attempt to pay it back.

Samantha honors her older brother Mickey with a gift. But as soon as he unwraps it, he gushes to tell her, "I am going to give you my old truck. I do not need it." Mickey could have thanked his sister and brushed off the urge to pay back her generosity.

Our gratitude frees us to honor givers and others at a time of our choice. Paul said to the Colossians to be rooted in Jesus, and they would overflow with thankfulness. "Rooted and built up in Him strengthened in the faith as you were taught and overflowing with thankfulness" (Colossians 2:7).

4. Love cancels the debt

The love motive directs us to forgive. We continue treasuring offenders and absorbing the personal impact of their offenses. We free offenders (and ourselves in the process) from emotional debts. First Corinthians 13:5 says, "Love keeps no record of wrongs." We go a step further and reconcile with willing others and build new trust. First Corinthians 13:7 says, "Love always trusts."

When our motive for giving is love, we aren't like the host in Proverbs 23:6: "Eat and drink he says to you, but his heart is not with you." Love gives freely, and that helps us grow in trusting God. We need to balance generous giving against safeguarding our identity. The result is that we prosper. Proverbs 11:24 says, "One person gives freely, yet gains even more; another withholds unduly, but comes to poverty." Jesus commended the widow for her faith and free giving despite her poverty (Mark 12:44).

5. Love hopes

Love and hope are relational experiences. Love hopes (1 Corinthians 13:7). It inspires hope in the beloved. Inspiring hope in the beloved through the *distinctness lens* means we respect the realities of time and place. We work with the beloved on what is doable here and now. We refuse magical solutions that circumvent reality because they make the heart sick (Proverbs 13:12).

Belinda wants a breakthrough in her finances. She thinks about buying a lottery ticket. Her friend Michelle tells her, "You are a creative cake baker. The breakthrough can be had by taking your current business to new markets!"

Through the *integration lens*, we inspire in others the hope of integration through grace. The outrageous grace favors them as a whole and covers their trespasses. Romans 11:6 says, "And if by grace, then it cannot be based on works; if it were, grace would no longer be grace."

When we relate through the levelness lens, we present the hope of commemorating self-worth through equality relationships. It is the hope that relinquishes the mad pursuit of wealth and prestige. It recognizes how our worth puts us on the same level as others. Through levelness, we hope to celebrate life in small and big ways.

In conclusion, the love motive manifests as loving behavior when we relate through the sound lenses of distinctness, integration, and levelness. Mischaracterizing the love motive or relating through distorted relational lenses causes us to behave hurtfully, even harmfully.

We need to submit our distorted perceptions of love to the Source of love. His Spirit and attitude dwell in us and will counsel us to love in the same manner He did.

Paul received an extraordinary deposit of love on the road to Damascus. I borrowed many of his characterizations of love from First Corinthians 13.

Love is intertwined with faith. It should not come as a surprise. Trusting God will lead us to receive His agape love and therefore love others. Second Thessalonians 1:3 says, "We ought always to thank God for you, brothers and sisters, and rightly so, because your faith is growing more and more, and the love all of you have for one another is increasing."

Paul concludes in 1 Corinthians 13:13 (AMP) that love, faith, and hope are related, but love takes the crown: "Now there remain faith, hope, love, these three; but the greatest of these is love." But love has different types. They are distinct, and each has its own magical flavor.

17

Flavors To Choose From

Same Motive, Different Relationship

"Milk is on the way, honey!" Kemisha says. She pours milk into the colorful cereal bowl for her toddler. She is a single mother who works two jobs to provide for him. She sits with him, delighted to watch him chewing cereal (not to mention making a mess!). She walks him to his preschool bus just in time to get picked up.

Back in her small condo, she sits on her old sofa. She sips her green tea and opens the Bible app on her phone. She reads and meditates. She pauses, her arms stretched to receive her heavenly Father's embrace.

Her phone rings as she gets ready to leave for work. Laurie, her friend, wants to meet for a weekend dinner. She and Laurie grew up together in the neighborhood. The two friends supported each other as they shared precious memories and made new ones.

On her subway ride, she gets a text with a heart emoji. It comes from Jackson, a man she is dating. He is done with his night shift at the factory. In her mind, she pictures his broad shoulders and salt and pepper hair as she reads his text.

In the last chapter, we addressed the fact that love is more than a feeling. It is a motive with specific moral fingerprints of honoring, protecting, telling the truth, forgiving, and hoping. This motive then directs our dealings with others through the lenses of distinctness, integration, and levelness. Like Kemisha, we engage in various types of love relationships every day. Each one operates differently and has unique functions. But all of them are guided by the love motive.

1. The parental love relationship (motherly love)

Infants are born with a fragile and desperate need for love. They can't verbally communicate, so they cry and kick. We should take the initiative to love them. Parental love provides care and connection.

It is vital to be physically present at birth to give bonding a solid start. We hold them in our arms as soon as possible and look into their eyes. We address them with their name and speak tenderly to them. We recite to them words of fondness, honor, and encouragement.

We comfort them with our words and embrace them in the midst of fear or hurt. We celebrate them daily, rejoicing in every new task they perform. We aim for our actions and words to register with them as love perceptions, so they always feel loved. Once they store enough love deposits, they feel loved even in our absence. Then they are ready to venture out and explore boundaries.

We want to affirm our love for toddlers when they say no. We don't attempt to change it to yes. Their no is their way to differentiate themselves and form their identity. We want to focus on keeping them safe and giving them options. We want to relate to teens increasingly through the distinctness lens. We aim to balance loving teenagers against transferring responsibility to them. Our love fortifies them, so they can take on more.

One of parental love's functions is to discipline children. Hebrews 12:6 says, "Because the Lord disciplines the one he loves, and he chastens everyone he accepts as his son." Discipline can take the form of letting children experience the consequences of their actions. It is better to plan the discipline and inform the teen about it beforehand. We should stay connected with them during the discipline and step in with further interventions if the experience becomes harmful. Romans 13:10 (TLB) says, "Loves does no wrong to anyone."

We should never judge, shame, or withdraw love when our teenagers offend or behave irresponsibly. Our continued love liberates them to experience consequences as a result of choices and not punishments. Colossians 3:21 says, "Fathers, do not provoke your children lest they become discouraged."

We cannot bestow on our children what we don't have. We need to have bonded in love and become responsible before we can demonstrate these attributes through our parenting. We aim for our youth to form their identity and become responsible for its disclosure. Success in education or career will follow.

Unlike romantic love or friendship, parental love lacks equality at the beginning. However, it encourages equality as teens mature and come out from under authority to adopt an equal position with us. We then relate to them as friends through the *levelness lens*. In Matthew 12:48, Jesus' mother and brothers asked to speak with Him while He was teaching. He replied, "Here are my mother and my brothers."

Leveling with parents does not put away honoring and serving them when they are in need (Exodus 20:12). It means that we and our grown-up teens are equal and free adults. They can stand up to, disagree with, and even confront us in love.

Parental love inspires hope in children. It is the hope that claims self-value through love relationships. It rejects achievement as the source of self-value and protects children from this disillusionment.

2. The friendship relationship (phileo or brotherly love)
Friendship is the main venue for relational life. Our friend-

ships meet our needs for listening, understanding, and empathy. We tend to befriend those with similar backgrounds, interests, and beliefs. As we form an identity and become responsible for our care, interests, and beliefs, we increase the prospect of befriending others. Our pursuit of growth attracts those who are growth-minded. Psalm 119:63 says, "I am a friend to all who fear you, to all who follow your precepts."

We look for signs of responsibility and freedom in new friends. Once we discern their trustworthiness, we initiate building trust and divulging ourselves. We want our credibility to invite our friends' trust and disclosure. Friendships with mutual self-disclosure can become quite deep. Proverbs 18:24 says, "But there is a friend who sticks closer than a brother." Each friendship, however, affords a certain depth of disclosure.

Relating to the *distinctness lens*, we respect our friends' views and don't try to change them. Mike and James are coworkers in an apple orchard. Mike hates jogging alone, so he asks James to join him after work. James thanks his friend but since he does not enjoy running, he declines to join. Mike respects his friend's refusal and continues jogging alone.

We are not responsible for pleasing our friends but for honoring them and speaking truthfully. While love does not harm, our friends may perceive our candid feedback as hurtful, especially when it exposes their hidden myths. Proverbs 27:6 says, "Faithful are the wounds of a friend, but the kisses of an enemy are deceitful."

Approaching friends through the *integration lens*, we accept them as a whole even when we witness their flaws. We have no illusions; we know integration takes time and abundant grace.

Relating through the *levelness lens* is a fundamental trait of friendship. We are equal to our friends. Each of us can stand with or up to the other. We support them in their tribulations yet oppose their vices.

It is prudent to have a handful of trustworthy friendships so we can distribute our needs for support and empathy among them. Trying to meet all our needs within a single friendship would probably suffocate that friendship.

Friendship is vital, but nurturing friendships during romantic relationships is even more so. When we observe our romantic partner's interactions with their friends, we recognize the partner's relational growth better. Romantic relationships are narrow in function. Alone, they don't support enough hearing, understanding, and empathy, while friendships can. We should never abandon friendships at the outset of a romance. It is precarious to endure the demise of romance without the support of trustworthy friends. Ecclesiastes 4:10 says, "But woe to him who is alone when he falls for he has no one to help him up."

3. The romantic relationship (*eros* love)

Romance is intoxicating. We idealize our romantic partners and lavish them with our attention and affection. We adore their physical details like body, eyes, and voice. Our affection broadens to include the small elements of their existence. I encourage you to read Solomon's description in Song of Songs 4:1:"Oh, how beautiful! Your eyes behind your veil are doves. Your hair is like a flock of goats descending from the hills of Gilead. Your teeth are like a flock of sheep just shorn."

In idolizing the beloved, we lay our guard down and seat them on our throne, emotionally speaking. We long intensely for intimacy with them and contemplate crossing any barriers to meet them personally.

Romantic feelings are a potent mix of adoration, excitement, and power. Once intoxicated by romance, we look and act differently, and our friends will quickly notice!

The emotional flood we feel, arising from knocking down boundaries and sharing intimacy, recedes after weeks or months.

We regain the distinctness lens and perceive the beloved's separate views and beliefs. We begin to discern their drawbacks and no longer consider them as perfect as we once did. With romantic feelings receding a bit, we need to relate to the beloved through the integration lens. We need to listen wholeheartedly and exchange thoughts with them to form goals together and accomplish things. As we succeed in this exchange, we become friends with our romantic partners. It is an effortless transition when romantic love caps friendship.

Romantic love is monogamous! It is limited to one partner at a time. This exclusive nature of romantic love, coupled with the physical connection, paves the way for the function of reproduction and rearing offspring.

Selma and Nick are classmates who grew up together. They are well acquainted with each other. During a group outing to the Jersey shore, Nick senses romantic feelings toward Selma. He reaches out to hold her hand, and to his delight, she reciprocates! The two decide to date exclusively.

Scripture balances honor with submission in marriage. Man occupies the leadership position and levels with the woman. He loves her as an equal and respects her life pursuits. First Peter 3:7 says, "Husbands, in the same way, be considerate as you live with your wives, and treat them with respect as the weaker partner, and as heirs with you of the gracious gift of life." The woman submits in freedom: "Now as the church submits to Christ, so also wives should submit to their husbands in everything" (Ephesians 5:24).

It can be challenging to comprehend how husbands and wives are equal, but the man leads. We need to approach this through the levelness lens, like Paul's description of Jesus in Philippians 2:6: "Who, being in very nature God, did not consider equality with God something to be used to his own advantage."

Romantic relationships are risky. The early tidal wave of romantic feelings can blind us to the beloved's flaws. It is better to date someone from our trustworthy friends (if possible) and let that relationship develop into a romantic one.

Pursuing romantic love from an emotional void is dangerous. We shouldn't marginalize our other friendships during romance. They are as valuable as ever in providing hearing, truthfulness, and encouragement.

4. *Agape* love relationship

God doesn't just love; He is love. "Whoever does not love, does not know God, because God is love" (1 John 4:8). The Holy Spirit bestows the Father's love without any merits. Romans 5:5 says, "And hope does not put us in shame because God's love has been poured out into our hearts through the Holy Spirit, who has been given to us."

God is free and does not violate our free nature. We are free to receive or reject His love. John 1:13 says, "Yet to all who did receive him, to those who believed in His name, He gave the right to become children of God."

We can love because God loved us first. First John 4:19 says, "We love because he first loved." The father initiated His agape love relationship to adopt us as children, not paid hires. We become empowered to love our neighbors and enemies alike.

As we fellowship with the Holy Spirit, He imparts to our mind His perceptions of honor and affirmation. He gently dismantles our barricades of fear and castles of doubt.

A life of gratitude is only possible after we receive agape love! It broadens our insight through the futility of covetousness, manipulation, and control. We cannot help but join in praising Him.

18

Repairing the Breach

An Offense Is Relational

Nicole tosses and turns in her bed. She replays in her mind what happened between her and Jonathan, her husband. They were high school sweethearts. He was a popular footballer, while she was a pretty and somewhat permissive girl. Jonathan had always related to Nicole through the devaluation lens, constantly dictating every aspect of her life. Nicole, seeking to keep the peace, avoided confronting him. She resented the degrading treatment but denied it in front of family and friends. The childless marriage had cracks that widened over time due to Jonathan's violence.

Fast forward to a few days ago. Jonathan came home from a late outing with his friends, and an argument about finances ensued. Jonathan got angry and slammed a salsa jar against the kitchen wall. Nicole felt terrorized and headed to her parent's house.

Nicole spent several sleepless nights weeping and praying. She finally made up her mind. She sat at the computer desk in her father's office. As the computer fan whirled, Nicole drafted an email to Jonathan. She conveyed her need for safety. She affirmed her love for him and intended to forgive him for the violence. She willfully bore the pain and sadness his violence inflicted on her. She confessed her compliance and wanted to attend a Christian counseling program about assertiveness.

Jonathan replied that he missed her and felt ashamed about his actions. He voiced his frustration with himself and wanted to see a therapist for his anger.

Despite Nicole dropping the domestic violence complaint, Jonathan faced civil penalties. Nicole was delighted that Jonathan enrolled in an anger management program. She sensed genuine signs of his taking responsibility. She declared her intentions to rebuild trust and reconcile with him.

Offenses are relational. Someone said it takes two to tango; it also takes two to offend. Both relational parties contribute to an offense. We may get offended without the other party intending to offend, such as with misunderstandings. But many offenses are deliberate, stemming from wicked intentions like pride, fear, and shame that induce us to devalue others.

We first offend others with our implied intentions before we do it in words and deeds. Jesus warned that intentions are the roots for the offense. Matthew 5:28 says, "But I tell you that everyone who looks at a woman lustfully has already committed adultery with her in his heart."

Our relational attitudes or lenses are crucial in inflicting and preventing offense. Relating through sound relational lenses helps us treasure others and respect their freedom, independence, and equality. When we relate to others through distorted lenses, we offend them. "Good understanding wins favor, but the way of the transgressor is hard" (Proverbs 13:15).

When we offend others, we can hurt and harm them. We breach trust and create a division in the relationship. Left unattended, the division robs the relationship of security and vulnerability, causing the demise of love. That is why Jesus cautioned about offenses, calling them stumbling blocks: "Jesus said to his disciples, things that cause people to stumble are bound to come, but woe to everyone through whom they come" (Luke 17:1).

Forgiveness Is Relational

We are instructed to forgive others in both the Old Testament (Leviticus, 19:18) and the New Testament (Matthew 6:14). Forgiveness is loving those who offended us and canceling their debts. It is a deliberate choice that is not begged for or demanded.

We begin to forgive by proclaiming the offender's worthiness of value and love. This is how God perceives them, and thus, how we ought to perceive them. The Holy Spirit imparts to our mind perceptions of love and worthiness about the offender. We need to agree with them and say it loudly. It is our agreement with those spiritual truths that frees us from the grip of offensive perceptions. It is the freedom that Jesus explained in John 8:32: "And you shall know the truth and the truth will set you free." His truth frees us to do the loving thing.

In the same way, an offense is relational, forgiveness is too. We obey the love motive and rehearse love for offenders through the lenses of distinctness, integration, and levelness.

Through the distinctness lens, we admit our presence during the offense and distinguish our share of how it transpired. We may not discern that others are aggressors or manipulative. "One who has unreliable friends soon comes to ruin" (Proverbs 18:24). We may have said no to irresponsible requests.

It is worth noting that compliance leads us to store frustration and resentment deep down, which cause us eventually to counter trivial offenses with destructive lashing out. Pilate Pontus acted in compliance when he failed to affirm his belief in Jesus' innocence. His offense was great, and according to most historians, he ended up committing suicide.

At first, we may be tempted to condemn offenders. But we have received Jesus' love and retired our inner judge: "Therefore, there is no condemnation on those who are in Christ Jesus" (Romans 8:1). We want to affirm our decision to forgive daily, even momentarily, and speak it in words. We lean on God and His saints for agape love and encouragement to continue the journey.

In relating to offenders as distinct individuals, we recognize that they have a free will and can potentially misuse it. Those who have not healed from their injuries often are the ones who misuse their will to injure others. We hold offenders responsible for their distorted thoughts and emotional outbursts. They are also accountable to the community for the financial and legal consequences of their offenses. Forgiveness does not relieve offenders from their civic responsibilities.

Through the distinctness lens, we won't withhold forgiveness from offenders until they change their ways. We are powerless to change them. We channel our power to safeguard our hearts and correct our myths.

Recognizing our distinctness, we take ownership of the offense's emotional impact. We absorb pain, sadness, and shame. We accept the added responsibilities related to healing and recovery. Our flesh will cry out for justice, but this is the time to approach God's throne for mercy and grace for our burning flesh. "Let us then approach God's throne of grace with confidence so that we may receive mercy and find grace to help us in our time of need" (Hebrews 4:16). We need to remember that God dispenses grace to us through His gracious saints. We cannot emphasize enough the importance of continually receiving love perceptions. We will reap healed emotions, but it is a late stop in the forgiveness journey.

Forgiving through the integration lens prompts us to give grace to offenders. They still have other virtues that we did not yet experience. We comprehend how they labor under the burden of wearing their masks. They offend in their pursuit to satisfy secret habits and addictions. Deep down, they are riddled with shame, living in constant fear of being exposed. They are not the stronger or happier people.

Through the levelness lens, we approach others who offend us as being worthy of love. We respect their freedom to choose when they relate to us through the disparity lens as their parents or children.

Forgive in Order To Heal

Forgiving is a journey that takes longer than expected. It is an emotionally taxing process and is crowned by our feeling better in the later stages. We forgive first in our thoughts, and then our emotions heal afterward. Forgiveness is the gateway to healing.

It is expected that we feel anger right after the offense. Yet Scripture cautions us about being angry with others personally: "But I tell you that anyone who is angry with a brother or sister will be subject to judgment" (Matthew 5:22). We need to deal with our anger by recognizing the demands we have as a result and verbally expressing them to God and wholehearted listeners. We can enlist God to help us meet worthy demands, like restoring privacy and being listened to and understood. In contrast, we will have to give up the unworthy or undoable ones, like changing what happened or demanding repentance from offenders.

Canceling demands hurts. Our perceptions construct our demands, which explains how they seem just to us. We can take the feelings of hurt and conclude that letting go is real. We need to surrender to the hand of the Gentle Potter. He gracefully does the reforming, so we adopt more loving and truthful thoughts.

We can consider the demands for justice only after we take responsibility for the initial wave of anger and pain. We need to perceive offenders as loved and worthy before setting out to seek civil or financial justice. We understand that justice is not a destination for vengeance but a step toward equality.

Sadness is sure to be felt after offenses. It is triggered by devaluation, the tearing of love bonds, and the breaching of trust. We enter the grief house and look up to the One who is acquainted with grief (Isaiah 53:3). We do not regret loving and trusting. Yet we need to embrace sadness, receive agape love, and own our choices. We can then use our new ways to relate more lovingly and share new joy.

We overcome the shame of offenses by receiving grace from God and His gracious saints. Only grace recipients can dispense grace (Ephesians 2:8). Turning to God will transform us to become like Him. Second Corinthians 3:18 says, "Being transformed into his image with ever increasing glory which comes from the Lord, who is the spirit."

Reconcile and Rebuild

Scripture tells us to forgive others and guard our hearts against their repeated offense (Proverbs 4:23). Those who relate through the distorted lenses of devaluation, splitting, and disparity repeat similar offenses. They don't know a freer, more responsible, or equal way of relating.

We guard our hearts by sharing less time and place with serial offenders. We can withhold sharing our thoughts or intentions with them, while we nurture deeper relationships with trustworthy, loving others. Paul instructed us in 1 Corinthians 5:9 not to associate with serial sexual idolaters because it lets offenders experience the consequences of being away from the loving fellowship.

Relating through the distinctness lens, we recognize our powerlessness to change offenders or demand their repentance. God takes no pleasure in the perishing of the offenders but in their repentance (Ezekiel 33:11). We need to continue to rehearse love perceptions towards them and consider reconciling with them when they repent.

God gave us the ministry of reconciliation through Christ. Reconciliation builds on forgiveness and renews relationships, risking new trust. Offense separates, forgiveness repairs the breach, and reconciliation brings us together as a community. Reconciliation is best approached through the *levelness lens*. We relate with offenders as equals. We clarify our intentions and invite them to declare theirs. We won't automatically resume trusting at the previous depth before the offense. We look for signs of responsibility and respect for equality as we slowly continue building trust. In conclusion, forgiveness is the work of love, and reconciliation is the crown of forgiveness.

God does not violate His nature. He is the Spirit of love and desires to dwell with loving spirits. Jesus recognizes how unforgiveness blocks the fellowship with the Father. He took the extraordinary step of asking us to pause our praying and go forgive them. Jesus said, "When you stand praying, if you hold anything against anyone, forgive them so that your Father in heaven forgives your sins" (Mark 11:25).

God operates through fellowship and performs miracles when fellowship becomes unity. No wonder Paul said in Philippians 2:2 (AMPC), "Fill out and complete my joy by living in harmony and agreeing and one in purpose, having the same love being in full accord and of one harmonious mind and intention."

Offenses divide Christ's body and distort God's calling. It is the devil's primary strategy to hinder the kingdom's work. We can't entirely avoid offenses, but we can minimize their occurrence by managing our differences with others and settling conflicts. It is a vital topic, so grab a coffee (or cappuccino!) and keep reading.

19

Duel of Wills

Conflict Is a Power Struggle

"Were you fighting with Aunt Hala?" Jack, my younger son, asked.

Looking into his curious brown eyes, I replied, "Not quite. I disagreed with her about a family matter."

Here is some context about the conversation. Our widowed dad, who lives abroad, recently met a woman he wanted to marry. He asked us to finance the wedding, but my sister opposed their marriage, while I supported it. The issue involved money, and we were trying to manage differences.

The conversation went like this:

"This marriage is a betrayal of our late mother," said my sister. "Besides, he is too old to start a family."

"I respect your view," I said. "I don't see him as disloyal. I don't believe he is marrying to have kids."

"I don't understand why he needs a wife. We can use the money to hire a caregiver for him."

"He told me he wanted someone he could age with gracefully. I thank you for trusting me with your views. At the same time, I intend to support his decision financially."

Our conversation was civil and not heated. We did not attack each other, yet someone viewed it as a fight.

So what is conflict? And how is it different from a disagreement? Disagreement is seeing differently on issues, views, and beliefs. It can morph into a conflict when parties invest time, resources, and willpower against others to settle their disagreements. Paul wisely says in 1 Corinthians 8:9, "Be careful, however, that the exercise of your rights does not become a stumbling block to the weak." He clearly understood how parties did not see eye-to-eye on issues. Conflict reflects more investment in the issues from both parties and sliding into a power struggle.

Failure to manage conflicts gives rise to divisions, arguments, and strife. The emotional toll is staggering; we wade into a swamp of frustration, disappointment, and anger. Solomon says in Proverbs 17:1, "Better is a dry morsel with quietness and peace than a house full of feasting with strife and contention."

Relationally, unmanaged conflict takes bites off the love bonds, devastating the relationship and leading to alienation, aversion, and hatred. That is why Paul warned the church in 1 Corinthians 12:25: "So that there should be no division in the body, but that its parents should have equal concern for each other."

False Views about Conflicts

Conflicts are a natural part of relationships, and we can argue that a conflict-less relationship is unequal or dishonest. When we approach conflicts through sound relational lenses, we can see an opportunity for increased responsibility and power. In contrast, when we view conflicts through distorted lenses, we perceive threats, failures, and impossible missions.

So what are some of the false views about conflict?

1. Conflict is a battle

When we relate through the *splitting lens*, we perceive conflict as a fight between good and evil. Shame motivates us to prove we are correct, and as such, we pursue winning at all costs.

In contrast, the love motive guides us through the *integration lens* to treasure others more than winning. Jesus, while on the cross, was taunted by teachers of the law, challenging Him to come down from the cross (Mark 15:29). Jesus loved them more than He wanted to win and prove them wrong. It is Jesus' love, not the nails, that pinned Him on the cross.

It is not unreasonable to yield to others who value winning too much, but if we do it through the *compliance lens*, we lose our freedom to be authentic. We need to speak our truthful minds to others as we yield. In doing this, we prevent frustrations, disappointments, and erosion of our identity.

2. Conflict is a threat

When we relate through the *devaluation lens*, we value things more than individuals. As a result, we see in the conflict a chance to lose or win items. We resort to manipulation and control to settle differences. Jacob used manipulation to resolve the conflict over the blessing of his dying father, Isaac (Genesis 27:10).

Fear drives us to avoid conflict altogether, but disputes that are avoided stay unresolved and produce strife. In strife, we unilaterally pursue desires and needs at the expense of love and care. Strife exhausts parties and usurps the relationship's resources, shattering it entirely. Proverbs 20:3 says, "It is to one's honor to avoid strife, but every fool is quick to quarrel."

3. Conflict is impossible to resolve

When we adopt this myth, we wave the white flag, we abandon our concern for others, telling them the truth, and inviting responsibility. First Corinthians 12:25 says, "So that there should be no division in the body, but that its parts should have equal concern for each other."

Through the *levelness lens*, we perceive others as equal, commit to managing the conflict with them, and refuse to flee before resolution.

Triggers of Conflict

Conflict is a natural occurrence. Let's examine its triggers and eliminate as many as we can. Prevention of conflict is much more prudent than management.

Some triggers are unavoidable such as life transitions. We may experience changes in health, finances, and employment. But even with those changes being out of our hands, we are still responsible for renewing our minds from myths and relating through the sound lenses of *distinctness, integration,* and *levelness.*

Myths are false beliefs that influence our perceptions of conflicts and other life topics. Our parents passed some myths to us through their parental love for us, while we form some myths through our relationships and life experiences.

Here are some of the important myths that can trigger conflict:

1. Love has qualifiers

In this myth, we set qualifiers for loving others, like getting payback or compliance. Those who harbor this illusion of care for others attempt to collect the qualifier. Freedom is the fine thread between love and control. Qualifiers often erase the line. Loving others unconditionally can be costly. That is why we should balance loving others with safeguarding our hearts.

The motive of love guides us through the *levelness lens* to love others because they are worthy. We hope our love will propel them to experience gratitude and, in turn, love others. There are no guarantees of how they will respond.

Jesus set no qualifiers for loving the disciples. He invited them to be adopted by His Father: "God destined us to be his adopted children through Jesus Christ because of his love" (Ephesians 1:5).

2. Change is a threat

Jack tells his friend, "You have changed. I feel like I am losing you. You have started a new friendship, and you don't spend time with me as you used to."

Jack perceives his friend's change as a threat that will cost him love. This is the second myth. Those of us who perceive change as a threat have not overcome fear. It could be fear of abandonment, loss of control, or provision.

Through the *distinctness lens*, we comprehend that others' freedoms entitle them to change. Their modification can be external, like getting new hairdos or piercings. Or it can be internal, affecting their attitudes and beliefs.

Faced with others implementing revisions, we want to request information about their motives for doing so. We want to know the process that led them to pursue change. If we assume others' motives for changing are malicious, we will fight off their alterations. They, sensing our push, will respond with defensiveness, and conflict will ensue.

When others perceive our personal changes as threatening, we can affirm them and disclose our motive for the changes. While some reassurances are appropriate, we won't alter our course due to their flawed perceptions. We are called to love others, not please them.

Paul clarified in Galatians 1:10, "Am I now trying to win the approval of human beings, or God? Or am I trying to please people? If I were still trying to please people, I would not be a servant of Christ."

Through the *integration lens*, we uphold others who are different as unique and applaud their individualism. It embellishes love and life. How boring life is when we are impostors of each other. In Jack's example, he needs to request more information, like saying, "I noticed you have a new friendship, and you are spending less time with me. Can you tell me more about your intentions? I value your friendship and want to understand you better."

3. Honesty is harmful

In the movie, *A Few Good Men*, a tough commander tells the military court, "You want the truth, but you cannot handle the truth." He assumes that his honesty will harm the military audience and hit their morale. His proud illusion causes him to lie, setting the stage for dramatic conflict.

The love motive guides us to speak our truthfulness to others, to illuminate their hidden illusions and sharpen their character. Our truthfulness kindly helps build the mature body of Christ. Ephesians 4:15 says, "Instead, speaking the truth in love, we will grow to become in every respect the mature body of him who is the head, that is Christ." We want patience and discernment to choose the proper time for the sharpening.

4. Communicating is all logic

Zack and his wife discuss buying a new car. The wife unassumingly asks, "Can we get an electric SUV? My girlfriend loves her electric car."

He intensely dismisses her request—an electric SUV costs a fortune! His wife feels annoyed by his response and withdraws in silence.

Zack says, "Like it or not, purchasing an electric car and installing a charger costs close to seventy thousand dollars, and it is way above our budget."

The wife sighs in resentment. "I no longer want a new car."

Their conversation spirals quickly into an argument.

Zack uses logic to confer facts about the exchange but doesn't sense the emotional content of it. He focuses on the accuracy of facts and disregards tenderness, understanding, and acceptance.

Our self resembles a house that is composed of logic and feelings. Logic represents the building structure, while emotions depict the furnishings and decor. When we relate through the *integration lens*, we employ logic and emotions together in communication.

The same Jesus, who said He is the truth (John 14:6), was moved by compassion when He saw the crowds helpless in Matthew 9:36. Jesus manifested truth and compassion in His relationship with others.

Jesus faced conflict daily as He traveled to preach the good news. He didn't fear conflict but saw it as an opportunity to preach the good news: "Let us go on to the neighboring towns, so I may preach there also, for that is why I came. so he went through Galilee preaching in their synagogues casting out demons" (Mark 1:38-39).

Whenever Jesus visited a town, He went straight to the synagogues, knowing that conflict was inevitable with the teachers of the law. Those Pharisees were deeply entrenched in the old teachings, and Jesus had His work cut for Him.

Even more, we observe how He visited Pharisees' homes, dined with them, and engaged them. Jesus treasured others who were involved in conflicts. He kept himself focused on loving, not winning. He introduced us to combining love and truth as a way of confronting. Let's read about it.

20

Conflict Through the Relational Lenses

Family Feud

Beirut has beautiful sunsets and sandy beaches. One summer, I rented a chalet there and invited my family. On a lazy afternoon, everyone was napping, and I took an Uber to meet a friend away from the resort. While I was away, my brother woke up and felt annoyed by my absence.

When I returned, he asked, "Where did you go?"

"I went to meet Pierre," I said.

"I came here because you said you want to spend time with me. Then you leave me to meet some friends?"

"You were resting, and I used my time to catch up with an old friend."

"Why is it vital to see that friend on vacation?"

Feeling frustrated by his persistent questioning, I thought to myself, *He assumes that he owns my time.* I kept a calm demeanor and said, "I am grateful for your presence. My intention was not to ignore you. At the same time, I decide how to use my time and whether I share it with you."

My brother is a loving person who cares for the extended family back home. He had not established clear boundaries and struggled to relate through the *distinctness lens*. It was evident that he and I approached time from different perspectives.

We form our relational attitudes, or as we call them, lenses through our upbringings and life experiences. Receiving love and

141

truthfulness leads us to grow and relate through the sound lenses of distinctness, integration, and levelness. In the absence of love, we experience delays and form distorted lenses. We use our relational lenses, whether sound or deformed, to perceive conflict and plot resolution.

Conflict and the Abandonment Lens

When we receive enough love deposits, we perceive being loved and relate through the *bonding lens*. However, if we don't receive enough love perceptions, we connect through the *abandonment lens*.

The ability to relate through the bonding lens is vital during conflict. It allows us to stay connected to the conflicted parties, even as we withdraw to safety. It is the launch pad, so we resume interacting and dialoguing with others in an effort to settle the discord.

However, through the abandonment lens, we relate only to others who are present with us. We live in a constant state of fear of aloneness. As soon as we experience conflict with others, we contemplate leaving the relationship. By ceasing to connect to them, we squander the chance to give or receive love perceptions and honest feedback. This spells the end of the relationship. Facing conflict with the abandoners, we need to lean on trustworthy saints to receive love and empathy in case we experience abandonment.

Sara met Peter during a trip to Las Vegas and married him without courtship. During the first day of their honeymoon, she noted that all Peter wanted was to play video games. When she voiced her desire to be physically close, he told her to quit distracting him. Later that day, she found out he had checked out of the resort without telling her. She realized the colossal mistake she made in wedding him. She felt shattered as she packed her suitcase to fly back home alone!

God does not abandon us halfway, even when we misuse our freedom. He is rooted in His love and is faithful to see us through: "Being confident of this, that he who began a good work in, you will carry it on to completion until the day of Christ Jesus" (Philippians 16:1).If we sin, we should never stop seeking God. His arms are always stretched and will even fall on our neck and embrace us as soon as we turn to Him (Luke 15:20).

Conflict and the Distinctness Lens

When we form our identity, we relate through the *distinctness lens*. We recognize that some conflict triggers lie within our boundaries, making them our own. We comprehend how our myths and emotional outbursts ignite conflict. We stop blaming others for conflict occurrences.

We learn to free ourselves so we can take the responsibility of settling conflicts with others where we speak our truthful needs and feedback. We don't triangulate a third party, hoping they will read our situation, talk on our behalf, and devise a solution. We don't lay the responsibility of the solution at others' doorsteps.

Jesus encouraged us to make an effort to settle disputes before going out to the court: "As you are going with your adversary to the magistrate, try hard to be reconciled on the way, or your adversary may drag you off to the judge" (Luke 15:28).

When we are delayed in forming an identity, we relate through the compliance or *devaluation lens*. Our relationships are marred with the same conflicts happening again and again. We become so used to disputes that we might even create them to test our partner's loyalty!

Through the *compliance lens*, we accept total responsibility for triggering the strife. We feel deeply ashamed of conflict occurrence being made known. We condemn ourselves for division arising from our worthy needs. We withdraw from friction to keep the image of harmony while, deep down, we resent our relationship.

When we approach conflicts through the devaluation lens, we see others in conflict as an extension of our possessions. We pursue the things we want from them without any regard for their freedom or responsibility. We value winning the contest at any price, so we intimidate others into submission. We yell, threaten, and even commit violence to get our way. It is our way or the highway. We do not listen to others or afford them empathy and therefore don't receive their solutions.

We read in Nehemiah 6:9 how Tobiah and Sanballat tried intimidating Nehemiah so he would not rebuild Jerusalem's walls.

> Paul and Maria are a middle-class couple. Paul wants to trade his pick-up truck for a new hybrid one. Maria objects and says, "Your vehicle is only two years old. It is in excellent condition." Paul gives Maria a death stare and firmly replies by saying, "All my crew is driving better trucks. This is not up for discussion."

Paul values getting the new shiny truck more than he values hearing Maria. He uses intimidation to cast his desire as an urgent need.

In relating through the devaluation lens, we resort to manipulation to manage conflicts. We often mislead and bait others. We hide our true intentions and exploit others' weaknesses to secure our needs or wants. We esteem the things we want more than we value others.

Jacob used manipulation to resolve the conflict over the blessing of his dying father, Isaac (Genesis 27:10).

Conflict and the Integration Lens

In receiving grace, we reconcile the inner good and evil leads and relate through the *integration lens*. We treasure others as unique despite encountering conflict with them. We extend empathy and grace to their shortcomings. We have been there and know the struggle is real. Jesus praises John the Baptist as "more than a prophet" (Mathew 11:9) even as the latter sent his disciples from prison to question whether Jesus was the Messiah or should they wait for another.

In relating through the *splitting lens*, we perceive others as a pinnacle of goodness until we encounter conflict over their flaws. We then perceive them catastrophically wrong and label them as untrustworthy.

The splitting lens not only makes it difficult to settle the conflict but also triggers conflict, namely, in two significant instances: our perception of others' anger and the refusal of our requests.

If we approach anger through the splitting lens, we fail to recognize others' constructive anger as a sign of their demands. We label them as angry individuals and perceive their anger as a personal attack.

Similarly, through the splitting lens, when others respond by saying no, we perceive their no as rejection. In reality, if they have rejected our request, we can take the request somewhere else. In Luke 9:54, Jesus sent messengers to the Samaritan village to prepare things for Him, but the town refused. While the disciples perceived rejection and asked to call for fire to destroy the town, Jesus rebuked the disciples and told them to take the request to another village. How gracious, our Lord!

Dianna had not reconciled her inner good and bad. She got engaged to James. She heaped praise on him in front of family and friends. One late night, she got into an argument with him after he suggested that she needs to be more financially separate from her family.

The next day, Dianna sent James a message, accusing him of greed. She terminated the engagement and kept the expensive ring. James was bewildered about the complete turnaround. Had he known about people who relate through the splitting lens, he wouldn't have been surprised.

Conflict and the Levelness Lens

Relating through the *levelness lens* enables us to value others as equals. Then we wouldn't perceive them negatively if we were to experience conflict with them. On the contrary, we look forward to being enriched by their gifts. Paul said in First Corinthians 7:7, "But each one of you has your own gift from God; one has this gift, another has that." We should respect others' attempts to persuade us and invite them to examine our views.

Through the levelness lens, we care about settling conflicts with others who may not be financially or vocationally accomplished. We perceive them as worthy and look to resolve differences in mutual respect. In Matthew 15:23, Jesus took time to settle the issue with a Canaanite woman. Since she wasn't a Jew, the disciples wanted to send her away, but Jesus leveled with her and healed her daughter.

Failing to level with others leads up to relating through the *disparity lens* where we perceive others we are in conflict with as all too powerful. We grovel and accept their request, sacrificing our truthful needs or wants.

This is the case with Mark and Mary, a married couple with children. Mark's parents are financially self-sufficient, but they keep asking Mark for money for various reasons. Mark doesn't recognize that he occupies the position of parental authority too and is equal to his parents. He can unconditionally both honor them and refuse their selfish requests.

Conversely, when we perceive others with whom we are in conflict as inferior, we belittle them. We don't think they are level with us, and we mock and accuse them. We are convinced that their views are wrong. In 1 Samuel, 17:28, Eliab, David's brother, looked down on him and accused him: "When Eliab David's oldest brother heard him speaking with the men, he burned with anger at him and asked: why have you come down here, and with whom did you leave those few sheep in the wilderness? I know how conceited you are and how wicked your heart is."

Relating through the *disparity lens* is a magnet for conflict. It induces us to submit to the person, not the position of authority. As a result, it causes us to rebel against authority when the position is occupied by a leader we disapprove of. Paul warned the Corinthians about loyalty to him or Apollos: "Do not go beyond what is written. Then you will not be puffed up in being a follower of one of us against the other" (1 Corinthians 4:6). Paul recognized how loyalty to a person is a form of pride, and it breeds division and more conflicts.

In conclusion, our relational lenses influence the way we approach conflict. They can help us care enough to resolve the problem or trigger more of it. No wonder Paul said in 1 Corinthians 13:11, "When I was a child, I talked as a child, I thought as a child. I reasoned as a child. When I became a man, I put the ways of childhood behind me."

We want to become relational adults who see conflict as an opportunity to sharpen each other (Proverbs 27:17). However, the sharpening cannot be done without love, although that may seem like a conundrum.

Loving others and confronting them at the same time? Yes! This is the subject of the next chapter.

21

Resolve and Reconcile

Resolve Rather than Manage Conflict

"I don' t want my name to be listed as a donor," I told Mr. Moussa, who was a missionary pastor from Africa. He was raising funds to install street lights powered by solar panels.

He said, "The project will bring lights to dark streets. It will reduce crimes and traffic accidents."

"It is a great cause," I said. "Count me in. But I do not want my name published on the project's social media site."

"I do not understand why. People may be inspired to donate more when they read the list of donors from the United States."

"I respect your view. A few may be inspired, and others may be discouraged. Some do not trust what they read on social media."

"Hmm . . . Okay, tell me more."

"I believe keeping donor names private gives God the glory. Also, it may cause the local folks to assume that their neighbors are also chipping in and helping. That would be amazing!"

We went back and forth on the issue. It became clear that Pastor Moussa relied more on social media to prompt ministry donations. I, on the other hand, believed the right hand should not know what the left hand gave. Both of us agreed on the donation cause, but we saw differently about the delivery details.

If you are curious how it ended, I donated to the project, and the pastor published the list of donors. He inserted "undisclosed name giver" instead of my name. (Yay!)

When it comes to settling conflict, we can never guarantee resolution. But we can consistently follow the proper order to attempt to resolve it. We can manage it more than fix it.

Managing the mental struggle that stems from incompatible or opposing needs, wants, or demands of others is the pinnacle of relational growth. We need to utilize all learned skills like ownership of emotions, wholehearted hearing, and dialogue. The love motive has to guide our relating through the sound relational lens by following steps in the proper order.

Philippians 2:3-5 says, "Do nothing out of selfish ambition or vain conceit, rather in humility value others above yourself. Not looking to your own interest, but each of you to the interests of others. In your relationships with one another, have the same mindset as Christ Jesus."

The Proper Order

Managing conflict requires following steps in a specific order. We walk the steps and hope to arrive at a mutual resolution. An ideal solution is an increase in responsibility and enrichment.

A proper order begins with ownership of emotions and treasuring others before disclosing views and inviting changes. The order goes as follows:

1. Ownership of emotions

Our emotional state at the outset of conflict dramatically impacts us. Perceiving conflict triggers frustration, anger, or fear. The first step is to acknowledge what we feel. We need to rest and appraise our emotions. We neutralize their power by expressing them to concerned listeners and receiving empathy and truth. Spilling our emotions aggravates the discord. If we fail to verbalize anger before the conflict, we find it seeping through our expressions. We may find our choice of words is poor, even degrading, during the exchange. Our nonverbal communication can be stern and inflections loud.

We need to acknowledge our own feelings, so we can do the right thing despite others' reactions. The psalmist depicts this vividly in chapter 119 verse 51: "The arrogant mock me unmercifully, but I do not turn from your law."

Through the *distinctness lens*, we know we can stay secure within our boundaries no matter how others react. No wonder Proverbs 16:32 says, "Better a patient person than a warrior, one with self-control than one who takes a city."

2. Choose a time and place

Delaying addressing others until we have control of our emotions is crucial. Once we can speak about the differences without becoming animated with feelings, we can plan meetings with the conflicting parties. The delay permits others to contain their emotions too.

We need to ignore the urge to expedite the scheduled meeting. We continue to seek our trustworthy friends for their truthful feedback about the differences confronted.

We confer with the conflict party to select the location for the meeting. The place has to be emotionally impartial for both parties. We can offer our choice or consider others' choices.

Those who relate through the *devaluation lens* try to control or manipulate the location or timing. Manipulators may attempt to lure us into their choice of location. In Nehemiah 6:10, Shemaiah tried to manipulate Nehemiah into going in a certain area: "Let us meet in the house of God inside the temple, and let us close the temple doors because men are coming to kill you."

Manipulators may attempt at the last minute to change the time just to be more in control. If we don't see any factual reason for this change, we should respond by affirming the chosen time.

3. Meet and exchange.

Having finalized the time and location, we focus on the meeting to exchange views and intentions. We need to maximize the exchange with conflict partners while still honoring them. That is done through conveying information with statements and gathering information with responsible questions.

In relating through the *distinctness lens*, we use the pronoun *I* to express our views, intentions, and needs. The word *I* clarifies separateness and responsibility for self. We also recognize others as distinct and won't use the pronoun *you* and attempt to read their mind or declare their intentions. It is better to say, "I want to understand more," versus "You do not make sense to me."

By inviting others to verbalize their intentions, we refuse to assume the knowledge of their motives. We affirm our awareness that events could have occurred without their intention. We free them from the assumption of having ill will toward us. First Corinthians 4:5 says, "Therefore judge nothing before the appointed time, wait until the Lord comes, he will bring to light what is hidden in darkness, and will expose the motives of the heart."

When we inform others about our perceptions and intentions, we trust them with part of ourselves. It is a risky but necessary move because we recognize the conflict as an opportunity for growth.

We gather information from others by asking questions. The responsible use of questions invites input from others about their needs, views, and intentions. We utilize open-ended questions that start with *when, what,* and *where.* They let others inform us about their journey leading to the present moment. We avoid the questions that are answered with *yes* or *no*. These questions lead others and reduce the information shared. We can see the difference between saying, "What experiences shaped your belief into a pro-life one?" and "Are you pro-life?"

We refrain from asking why, as others may perceive their motives as being debated. We instead invite them to reveal their motives. We notice the difference between saying, "Why are you silent? and "I did not hear any words from you. Please tell me what you want by being silent."

We are better off without hypothetical questions because they don't help us gather information about current views. Similarly, we respond to hypothetical questions by stating our current wants and intentions and inviting others to state theirs.

4. Value before feedback

The love motive guides us to treasure others before giving them our truthful feedback. Through the *distinctness lens*, we own the responsibility of sharing our feedback and respect others' responsibility for theirs.

Through the *integration lens*, we treasure others and value the journey that leads them to differ from us. Valuing others does not mean agreeing with their current views or actions. Romans 5:8 says, "But God demonstrates his own love for us in this: while we were still sinners Christ died for us." God does not wait for you to fix yourself before He values you.

As for the *levelness lens*, it lets us affirm others as equal and precious. Galatians 3:28 says, "There is neither Jew nor Gentile. Neither slave nor free nor is there male and female, for you are all one in Jesus Christ. If you belong to Christ, then you are Abraham's seed and heirs according to the promise." Affirming others is vital so they can tolerate the emotional toll of our truthful feedback.

Following our affirmations of them, we give truthful feedback focusing on facts and observations, avoiding assumptions. Notice the difference between saying, "I heard you cursing in response to your colleague's statement" and "Your colleague seems upset, and it looks like you swore at him."

Through the distinctness lens, we are free from the responsibility for others' feelings but responsible for being loving and empathetic. We invite others to express their truthfulness, so we can combine them with ours and therefore construct a complete relational truth.

Those who relate through the *devaluation lens* lie about their truthful feedback to further their selfish intentions. In contrast, those who relate through the *compliance lens* conceal their feedback to please others.

The *integration lens* enables us to link valuation and feedback by the word *and*. Notice the word *and* in the following sentence: "You are a hard worker, and I want you to show more kindness toward your subordinates." The *splitting lens*, on the other hand, uses the word *but* to unlink valuation and feedback. It tips the balance away from the valuation and singles out the flaws. Our previous sentence would change to: "You are a hard worker, but you are not kind towards your coworker."

Through the *levelness lens*, we give truthful feedback to correct misunderstandings and not to judge others or relate to them from above, like preaching or treating them as children. Luke 6:37 says, "Do not judge, and you will not be judged, do not condemn, and you will not be condemned. Forgive, and you will be forgiven." We need to deliver our feedback kindly in small installments. Giving considerable feedback exhausts others and is likely to be perceived as venting.

5. Invite change

Having given feedback and noting it was received well, we can invite others to share changes we model ourselves. Philippians 3:16 says, "Join together in following my example, brothers and sisters, and just as you have us as a model, keep your eyes on those who live as we do."

Through the *distinctness lens*, we comprehend that we are powerless to change others. They need to buy into the change and recruit their own resources.

Through the *devaluation lens*, some want to bring changes through intimidation or manipulation. That won't last.

Through the *integration lens*, we empathize with others who struggle to change. They toil with secrecy and feelings of shame and fear. We should celebrate their strengths, so they can overcome their flaws. Others change in small steps that may not be tangible to us; we need forbearance and self-control and should administer grace and encouragement to them.

Perhaps there is no better way to invite change than through the *levelness lens*. Levelness joins others together and affirms equality with them. Philippians 2:21 says, "For everyone looks out for their own interests, not those of Jesus Christ." Levelness pleads with others to become more loving and just.

A word of caution—we shouldn't demand from others to abruptly quit a particular behavior. That sinful behavior caters to specific needs or wants, and by suddenly stopping it, they could experience a vacuum that they may fill with even more risky behavior such as violence. The new responsible behavior should displace the old selfish one. There is no ceasing but rather displacing.

Settling conflict reshapes relationships to be more free, equal, and loving. From then on, we can express our intentions and lay down the cornerstone of a new trust. We shred the old files and resume the incredible work of reconciling.

God has reconciled us through Christ and given us the ministry of reconciling others to Himself. Second Corinthian 5:19 says,

God was reconciling the world to himself in Christ, not counting people's sins against them. And He has committed to us the message of reconciliation. We are therefore Christ ambassadors, as though God were making his appeal through us. We implore you on Christ's behalf: Be reconciled to God.

As Christ's ambassadors, we are on a collision course with conflict as we evangelize others. We want to honor and level with others before inviting them to the kingdom.

I hope and pray that you will overcome the adversity of conflict and usher many to the kingdom. Amen.

22

The Power of Presence

Face-to-face Is Better

"Guys, here I come again!" said the blonde lady featured in a documentary about dating. She was scammed by an online con who posed as a diamond dealer. It was emotional to watch how she was lured into spending her money as she chased love. Ironically, she concluded the episode by signing up on another online dating site again!

Social media has caused an earthquake in the way people live and communicate. They can connect in real-time using sound and pictures. I can video call my father, who works at his farm thousands of miles away, while I sip my coffee in front of the fireplace.

Social platforms offer unprecedented means of identifying new people and services. Some are across the street; others are across the ocean.

Mobile technological innovation permits social media apps in bedrooms, offices, even airplanes. Social media has effectively crossed time zones and erased the time boundary. Saying "Good morning" in the US is interpreted as "Good night" in Thailand. Fast communication allows the execution of many functions remotely. Software engineers or crypto investors work exclusively from home computers and rarely go to a physical work site.

The medical quarantine resulting from the Coronavirus pandemic has forced hundreds of millions to stay indoors, boosting the reliance on the internet and social media for scholarly and professional careers. Many join exercise regimens nowadays using smart connected bikes.

Looking back in time to when Jesus lived, He often traveled on foot to bring the good news. His trips between villages took hours and days. Jesus said the thief comes to steal, kill, and destroy (John 10:10.) The thief has not changed, but he is aided now more by the ease of trespassing on boundaries of time and place.

The Relational Risks of Social Media

Social media enables connections between people and services under the pretense of economic growth. Nonetheless, the improved access lowers the threshold of relational harm by permitting violations of boundaries easier than ever; offenders no longer need to be physically present with the offended.

Social platforms present a large sum of visual and audio expressions. However, many are assumptive. Users' posts reflect their reactions and the relational lenses they use to approach relationships.

Users often post perceptions and occasionally observations. They may not recognize the difference between perceived assumptions and observed facts. With postings going viral, presumptions vastly outweigh observations on the platform.

With emotions being responses triggered by either presumptions or facts, many take to social media to get their emotional fix. They crave the feelings of joy, excitement, and closeness away from the realities of lived relationships. They forget that the real treasure is the person sitting next to them. They chase after clouds that don't rain. Proverbs 25:14 says, "Like clouds and wind without rain is one who boasts of gifts never given."

Getting cash from an ATM does not make you rich, but productive work away from the machine builds wealth.

Browsing social media can be risky. And no, we are not talking about cyber risks! These are the following emotional risks:

1. The decline of self-worth

Time is not renewable and therefore is a limited commodity. We have a certain quota at our daily disposal. We need to budget generous amounts of time to be physically present to care for our loved ones and give them honor and gratitude. One of the best ways to showcase our care for them is by giving them attention and wholehearted listening. We want to hear their words, but more importantly, let them in emotionally.

Empathy can't be given in a hurry. It is a shared experience in which we come close to feeling what others feel. It helps them gain power and even delight as their struggles persist. Psalm 119:77 says, "Let your compassion come to me that I may live, for your law is my delight."

It is the receiving of love and gratitude within relationships with our close ones that enables us to experience self-value. Depriving those relationships of quality time will cut down the supply chain to self-worth.

A relationship with less time vested in caring becomes shallow and unable to withstand differences. The result is flourishing conflicts and strife. The relationship failure will deal severe harm to self-worth.

Laura is a busy professional. Her husband feels strongly about global warming. So when he stumbles upon an online campaign to fight drought, he joins immediately. But what started as a noble gesture snowballed into a significant commitment that consumed more and more of his time. Whenever Laura was with Ed, she couldn't get his attention because he was replying to the group's postings. She grew frustrated and hurt. She eventually firmly said, "We need quality time together!"

2. The unintended self-disclosure

We disclose ourselves to wholehearted listeners to get love and healing. The process is deliberate, mutual, and slow. We maintain ownership of our identity throughout the disclosure. In addition, as we disclose to those physically present, we receive their verbal and nonverbal content, and therefore meet our needs for understanding, empathy, and truth.

The same cannot be said about disclosure on social media. Whenever we post, we reveal part of ourselves to many recipients without determining their trustworthiness. Once we reveal enough pieces, we unintentionally disclose ourselves to the whole world web. Since we cannot receive recipients' nonverbal, we don't experience the benefits of wholehearted listening.

With the recipients of self-disclosure being untrustworthy, we risk betrayal, ridicule, and rejections. Consider the following scenario of betrayal:

> Pam shares her vacation pics with an online friend. Days after disagreeing with her friend over women's rights, she sees the images posted on the woman's page. With privacy settings set to the public, everyone has access to them.

Proverbs 18:24 says, "A man of many companions may come to ruin, but there is a friend who sticks closer than a brother." How much is too much? Most of us have online friends by the hundreds or thousands!

3. Social influence

Social influencing takes place when receiving virtual content causes a change in our perceptions. The change is real, albeit indiscernible on a day-to-day basis.

Those who don't guard their heart with all diligence (Proverbs 4:23) are the most influenced. They relate through the compliance lens and accept whatever online perceptions come their way. They adopt new diets, views, and beliefs. When they are not connected to reality, they may even conform to an entirely new identity away from trustworthy friends who love them and speak truthfulness to them. Paul cautions about conformity in Romans 12:2: "Do not conform to the pattern of this world, but be transformed by the renewing of your mind."

Entrepreneurs understand social influence well. They employ influencers to steer users toward their products and services. Social influencers have mustered large numbers of followers on social media. Backed by their popularity, they broadcast their perceptions to influence followers and others. They may steer others to vote for a candidate, follow a diet, or buy a service. Not all influencers are minions for entrepreneurs. Some have talents in education, nutrition, or spirituality.

Anyone who uses social media is subject to social influence, whether the platform is sponsored or free. We need to inspect the credentials of influencers using third-party references. Their sponsor could be a charity, college, marketing company, or government agency.

Whatever the social influence, it can quickly become an idol that turns us away from God. Jonah 2:8 says, "Those who cling to worthless idols, turn away from God's love for them." We must heed Jesus' words in John 15:9 and abide in His love.

The Responsible Use

When we relate through the *distinctness lens*, we grow in responsibility and freedom. We comprehend that social media is a tool we can use responsibly.

We can employ social media to deepen relationships, love, and serve others, but we need to be mindful of the following:

1. Building trust in the physical realm

Building trust dictates that we first distinguish the trustworthy others, which is much easier away from the virtual world. For example, we can examine others' behavior to ensure it aligns with their words. Paul said of Timothy in 1 Corinthians 4:17, "He will remind you of my way of life in Christ Jesus, which agrees with what I teach everywhere in every church." We can observe others' verbal and nonverbal interactions with their family and friends.

In contrast, building trust with virtual users is fraught with challenges. What we know about others is largely presumptive. Experiencing trustworthiness from others in the virtual world takes us on a long and twisted path. Having said that, we can use social media to deepen communication with others we have already built trust in the physical realm. This is especially useful when they are geographically distant.

David uses social networking messenger to connect with his dad, who lives in a different state. Those video conferences helped David and his family show their affection toward Grandpa. At the same time, it instilled in the aging man a sense of reward for experiencing his grandkids, love, growth, and achievements.

2. Limited self-disclosure

We need to review any visual and audio statements carefully before posting them. We should choose a trustworthy group or audience. Our truthful messages disclose various parts of ourselves. We need to keep in mind that the recipients of our content can rebroadcast it to anyone and everyone.

If we set the recipient of our content to the public, we lose ownership of the content; it becomes available to everyone out there. As a result we would've disclosed ourselves to many others and exponentially increased the risk of mistreatment, rejection, and ridicule.

Using social platforms is like using our tongues. It is best to limit self-disclosure on social media and do it only to our long-standing trusted friends. Proverbs 13:3 says, "Those who control their tongue will preserve their lives, but those who speak rashly will come to ruin."

3. Prioritize physical presence

Our physical world presence is far more effective in deepening relationships than through social media. It allows us to convey our nonverbal expressions and empathy.

We need to relate with our loved ones by being physically present. This way, we deepen our relationships with them and safeguard their self-value and ours. We can use a smaller portion of time to relate through social media with the recognition that it is an auxiliary way of relating and never the main one.

The virtual world is ineffective as a route for relationships. Genuine relationships dictate experiencing others in real-world encounters and observing their relating to others. Pursuing relationships through social platforms is shaky since we relate to others' virtual images, which may not represent them.

No amount of information here is enough to give complete answers for our lives and relationships. We need the guidance of the Holy Spirit. He counsels us about others with whom we fellowship. He helps us discern others' virtual content and affirm what honors, unites, and levels while rebuking what is oppressive, hateful, and divisive.

Our world has become technology connected. Fear falsely promises safety in exchange for withdrawal from technology. Second Timothy 1:7 says, "For God has not given us a spirit of fear but of power and love, and a sound mind."

Philippians 4:13 tells us, "I can do all things in Christ who empowers me." We can rein in social media and use it to further the kingdom, love, and serve. Amen.

Conclusion

One of my assets and (possibly flaws), is that I write with the purpose of giving information. As such, my writing tends to be dense with data. So, friends, if you are reading this conclusion, let me extend my congratulations to you for your perseverance. You have accomplished reading a book that is quite informative.

When growth is our goal, we find that it cannot be outsourced and often requires us to peel off layers of old perceptions and resultant attitudes. The word *attitude* in modern day parlance has become synonymous with negative behavior. Social media became aversive to the word and coined special names for people who have negative attitudes. However, whether we like it or not, each of us has our own attitude, which is part of ourselves, like our face, voice, and posture. To achieve growth, we need to become aware of and take ownership of our personal attitude. Nothing is more fulfilling than transforming our attitude or relational lenses. It reinvents how we present ourselves in relationships at work, in education, and in our leisure time.

A prudent application of using the relational lenses will yield insight in handling day-to-day interactions, their challenges, and our conflicts. We will see with clarity the lines of responsibility, freedom, and equality. Detecting stumbling blocks allows us to navigate around them or leap over them. With transformed relational lenses, we choose better words and phrases and take time to consider our words as fruits we present to our loved ones daily.

I want to share with you a practical application of each of the four lenses to sum up our concepts. The stories and characters are fictional, but I feel they are helpful to present relatable scenarios.

1. The bonding lens. Leslie was a lactation specialist checking on a mom who was nursing her newborn baby. The young mom was distressed over the difficulty in having her newborn latch onto her for breastfeeding. She tearfully told Leslie, "I feel like I am failing to love him." Leslie said, "It is a difficult feeling. At the same time, loving your baby is far more than just breastfeeding. It is gentle touches, deliberately looking in his eyes, and softly speaking with him. When breastfeeding takes longer than expected, remind yourself to use that time to enjoy giving him those loving deposits." The young mother's eyes brightened and she nodded. Leslie concluded, "I commend you on your breastfeeding efforts. I want you to connect more and enjoy this wonderful experience."

2. The distinctness lens. Joe works at a used car dealership. A customer came to the dealer, test drove a van, and considered buying it. Albeit being a young salesman, Joe had formed his identity and related through the distinctness lens. He shared with the customer how the van would meet his family needs. Then he offered the customer an extended warranty. He said, "Repairs can be expensive down the road." The customer declined the offer. Joe pressed ahead explaining how the responsibility of repairs can be expensive and inconvenient. "When I sell you the car, I hand over the responsibility of its maintenance to you. I want your family experience to be safe and pleasant." The customer's face relaxed. Joe added, "I can give you a discount on it. Think about it for few minutes while I get you a cup of coffee." When Joe returned, he found that the customer had decided to buy the extended warranty. Joe's words showed his respect for the customer's freedom and highlighted the lines of responsibility. That netted him the sale. Kudos, Joe!

3. The integration lens. During a professional football game, Coach Peter substituted his back liner and drew the ire of the player. He stared down his coach and let out a loud frustrated slur. Peter, being the authentic person he was, viewed the incident through the integration lens. The coach did not view the player's anger as a personal attack on him. He saw the whole picture and realized this linebacker's anger was part of his emotional side as an individual. It reflected his demand to compete and win. The player has other great parts of him, such as being a tough, smart and disciplined defender. Peter responded to the player's anger with a steady eye contact and thanked him for his effort. Peter's composure on the field won him the respect of commentators and spectators alike. His team went on to win. During the press conference afterward, he brushed off the incident and celebrated his team's victory.

4. The levelness lens. Christina was involved in a conflict with her husband over their financial management. The couple sought help from their local church. During the meeting, the church elder asked Christina to submit to her husband as the Bible teaches and added, "Your husband is the house leader." Christina was deeply rooted in God's love and understood her worth in Him. She was also aware of her rights and freedom in Christ. She told the pastor she would submit to her husband as long as he managed his leadership role responsibly to safeguard the household, but she would refuse to submit when he mismanaged money and committed financial infidelity. Christina saw through the Levelness lens that she was equal with her husband and with the pastor. She could stand up to them if they misused their authority position. The pastor prayed for the couple, and he could not help but praise her brave and loving stance.

Beloved, God is a spirit. He desires to dwell in our earthy tents and manifests His love to others. It is our relational lenses that enable us to emit His love to others in a way that respects their freedom of responsibility and equality.

It is my prayer that you polish your lenses, so you begin seeing others as Jesus sees them. For then, your light will shine and illuminate others path towards your Father in heaven. Amen.

About the Author

NIDAL HUMOEE came to the United States to pursue medical training. Little did he know, he was the one who would be pursued by the Abba love.

He overcame brokenness through embracing love and truth. As an emotional overcomer, Nidal believes that relationships are venues for healing, maturity, and contentment.

Currently Nidal practices as a pediatrician at Hunterdon Health Care. He lives with his children in Clinton, New Jersey, where he enjoys paddling and gardening.